CONVERSATIONAL

PRAYER

CONVERSATIONAL PRAYER

A Handbook for Groups

Rosalind Rinker

WORD BOOKS, Publishers
Waco, Texas • London, England

To my sister
DENISE RINKER ADLER

and to all
who are willing
to use skill and gentleness
in teaching
the art of prayer

Acknowledgments

I gratefully acknowledge the competent help of Lorraine Carlson, whose assistance as to content and organization has been invaluable; the detailed labor of love by Sally Shideler Torrey, who prepared the list of supplementary readings found at the close of each chapter; the personal support of my friends Shirley Chalmers and William H. Ward during this time of writing; and the fine work of my editors, Floyd W. Thatcher and Mary Ruth Howes.

CONTENTS

✤ ✤ ✤

Part III. Guidelines for Growing Groups

Foreword

✤ ✤ ✤

We are surrounded by a new generation that is clamoring for truth and reality. Unless the style and format of our religious meetings are drastically changed, the church (as we know it) will soon be left with an aging generation clinging to old traditions—and no one coming up to take its place.

From my very first book on prayer, written in 1959, I have underplayed the case for conversational prayer in order not to alienate my fellow Christians but to gain their cooperation. I have urged, but not strongly enough, that traditional forms of monologue prayer be left with those who need them. I have poured out my heart to those who long to reach the silent worshipers among us. And there has been change. But much more needs to be done. We must help these silent ones become audible, help them break that sound-barrier of silence and teach them a simple, meaningful way of praying together. When we have done this we will have fulfilled the law of Christ: love one another.

Will you be one who dares to step out? Will you become a teacher of prayer and use these new and different ways to make Jesus real?

If you will, this handbook was written for you. It has been prepared for those who desire specific aids in teaching conversational prayer. It contains more than method, however. You will find it to be an outline on how to experience God's love, how to believe God loves you, how to release that love. It will help people discover what they can believe at a given

point, how they may develop prayer-power by agreeing together and affirming one another.

For more than ten years these four steps of conversational
prayer have been used by churches and taught in prayer workshops, many of which I have personally conducted. I have
seen groups of people, small and large, transformed (i.e. released by joy) in the first ten minutes of experiencing together just the first two steps: *Jesus is here,* and *Thank you,
Lord.*

You, too, can have this experience.

As I send these lessons to you who are daring to step out,
I commend you to the guidance of the Holy Spirit, who is the
great Teacher of us all.

ROSALIND RINKER
Chicago, 1969

How to Use This Book

In spite of repeated requests for this handbook, I hesitated a long time before I wrote it because method becomes outdated. It is the Holy Spirit, rather than mere method, who brings freshness and life through change.

And yet the need for teaching new methods of prayer is evident. Laymen are embarrassed and untrained to pray. They have little time for study, but they do have a desire to know how to pray together, how to relieve fear and anxiety, and how to realize the love of God.

Do not be deceived by the simplicity of this book. These methods do work. The assurance and love released to the participants in conversational prayer has for countless numbers been a life-changing experience.

CONTENTS

The book is divided into three parts. Part I defines the need for and the content of conversational prayer, including a chapter which sets the spiritual tone of the book.

Part II teaches the four basic steps of conversational prayer in a series of dry-run outlines which will give you details of procedure and purpose. Accompanying each step are many practical workshop helps along with chapter reviews and suggestions for supplementary reading from my first three books on prayer.

Part III contains guidelines for growing (or more ad-vanced) groups along with a list of subjects which further amplify the teaching of Part II.

The last section of the book contains an outlined bibliography and an index of subjects which is a valuable guide to locating information quickly.

FOR THE TEACHER

1. Part I should be read carefully for a fresh background in preparation for the detailed teaching coming up in Part II.

2. In Part II, a general lesson plan precedes chapters 4 and 5 which are to be taught as one unit. Another lesson plan precedes chapters 6 and 7 which form another teaching unit. Keep this in mind as you read, and it will help you in planning actual group sessions.

3. Parts I and II will give you an overall grasp of the subject for introducing the four basic steps of conversational prayer to your group.

4. Feel free to select what you need from the detailed instructions given. If you are not satisfied with your first session, go back again and see which instructions you missed . . . try it again.

5. You will need my three previous books on conversational prayer (see Abbreviations) for supplementary reading on various subjects.

FOR A TRADITIONAL GROUP

Changing from a monologue to a dialogue prayer-pattern can be done. Remember that one of the chief reasons for teaching a new form of prayer is to involve people, to bring them into a personal relationship with God, and to give them the freedom to love themselves and each other.

Use the helps provided in this book, and check the index and the supplementary reading suggestions for any problems you meet. An open discussion of the old forms and the barriers they present to non-audible "pray-ers" is advisable.

FOR ANY GROUP

Start a book-reading club. Paperbacks of my first three books on prayer are available, as well as a host of other fine books, some of which I have listed in the bibliography. Discuss and put into action what you read. Take turns leading. Evaluate what you are doing and why. Welcome all reactions. Learn to pray together by doing.

The most important thing is to take the first step toward learning to pray together. Make a start, but take it easy— pray for only five minutes at a time. The secret is to stop before people want to stop.

ABBREVIATIONS

The abbreviations I have used for my books on prayer are as follows:

I   = Book I = *Prayer—Conversing With God.*
II = Book II = *Communicating Love Through Prayer.*
III = Book III = *Praying Together.*
HB = this handbook = *Teaching Conversational Prayer.*

For bibliographical data on the first three books, see Bibliography, I, C.

PART 1

✠ ✠ ✠

Conversational Prayer Defined

Chapter 1

✤ ✤ ✤

THE NEED FOR TEACHING PRAYER

When I receive letters like those that follow, I know there are people who need not only the moral encouragement but the actual technical help which comes from "a book in hand" to guide them into new ways of teaching people to pray.

I am re-reading your book, *Praying Together*. When I came to the question, "Would you like to be a member of a class in training for leadership in teaching prayer?" I found myself saying, yes, yes . . . but *how,* dear Lord, *how?*

Mrs. C., *Australia*

The pastor of a Reformed Church writes:

Our church has come to a real awareness of the need for a new approach to prayer and small groups where people can meet each other and Jesus Christ in a new openness. However, as a whole our church has not caught the significance of this. We invite you to come to . . . . Church and share with us your insights and enthusiasm. This could be the spark needed to launch us into a greater program of outreach which we sense is so urgent at this time.

Rev. RHR, *Michigan*

That needed spark is being kindled in the hearts of many persons who are open both to being taught and to teaching old truths in a new way. Changes are due. Change is here. Let us not be afraid. Truth never changes, but to command attention, ways of expressing truth must change.

And yet something holds us back. Mrs. R., for instance, has assisted me in several prayer workshops, yet she hesitates to move out on her own. Recently she said, "We've just accepted a new pastorate—a large church which has the reputation of being a spiritual lighthouse in the community. And yet—those people don't really know how to pray together. They are still praying those lengthy, impersonal, Shakespearean prayers. And only a certain few take part."

"Why don't you get busy and teach them?" I asked.

She sighed audibly. "Oh, I know I should and I want to, because I can't stand what is going on when I know what *could* be going on. But . . . I don't seem to know where to start." Rather hopefully she looked at me. "Won't you come and help me?"

Not that I wouldn't like to. But why not Mrs. R.? What was her hang-up? Suddenly I knew. She needed confidence.

THE CONFIDENCE OF BEING EQUIPPED

Reading books and listening to lectures does not automatically make us able to teach others. When alone and away from the source of inspiration, we may need a special kind of help—the kind that comes from a special book of instructions right there in one's hand. In other words, people need a manual which will, in plain language, outline the first steps, and the next steps—a book which can be referred to again and again.

For certain types of people (maybe you are one of them) a book can provide the necessary confidence to move out and get started.

Or perhaps you are the opposite type. My files contain many wonderful letters from those who went out and taught others without a manual. There are some, who without special instruction, are using their gifts of enthusiasm and teaching. But not all of us are able to do this.

WOULD YOU LIKE TO TEACH PRAYER?

Would you like to pray with someone? Would you like to teach children to pray? Or teenagers? Or adults?

The resources are here for you—the detailed help you need.

How does an adult break old patterns? The methods are here.

Where does one start?

One starts with an understanding of the words of our Lord as recorded in Matthew 18:19, 20. The power of two or three agreeing in the presence of God opens the doors of love and healing to every human being and to every human need.

Prayer is one of the keys to growth and maturity.

To learn to pray is to experience the love of God released.

SUPPLEMENTARY READING
for Chapter 1

Book and page	Subject
I p. 44	Simple instruction brings results
III pp. 42-44	Need for training leaders
III pp. 47-52 (ch. 5)	Need for teaching prayer
III p. 72	Need for trained laymen

Chapter 2

✤ ✤ ✤

WHAT IS
CONVERSATIONAL PRAYER?

A DESCRIPTION OF CONVERSATIONAL PRAYER

What is conversational prayer?

How does it differ from traditional prayer?

Traditional prayer is a monologue, i.e., some person "leads" in prayer and others (presumably) listen. This type of prayer has been used in prayer meetings as long as any of us in this generation can remember (and by generations before us). The average traditional prayer meeting is attended by from ten to twenty persons, while only three or four of these pray audibly and usually at some length.*

The letters and requests quoted in chapter 1 contain a plea for help that is repeated constantly—help for rescue out of the deadness and dullness experienced in most prayer meetings.

Conversational prayer is an answer to these pleas for help.

---

*For an illustration, see Book I, pp. 16-17.

It has dropped the traditional patterns and adopted the open language of the heart: honesty, love, and simplicity. This is possible because of a fresh knowledge and awareness of God's love and presence.

Conversational prayer is a dialogue engaged in by people who are moving in love toward one another. Instead of only a few taking part, everyone is "with it" all the time.

Conversational prayer, however, is more than a dialogue. It is what its name implies. It is conversation directed to God with us and within us, as well as to each other. Therefore it contains three ingredients common to any meaningful communication:

1) *We become aware* of the other person, what he says, what he means, how he feels.

2) *We pursue the same subject* by taking turns, listening, speaking, agreeing, and giving thanks.*

3) *We try to keep in tune,* by not prematurely introducing a new subject, but by maintaining interest through participation in the current subject.

Prayer is thus lifted out of the cold, formal, impersonal routine (and the Shakespearean language) into the warmth of fresh, personal, everyday language—in the presence of Jesus our Lord who is always near us.

Those attending a traditional meeting are likely to go home feeling as fearful and unloved as when they came. Anyone attending a meeting where conversational prayer is practiced will surely go home feeling loved in spite of himself—with the citadel of fear, insecurity, and loneliness having been rocked to its foundations.

You may ask, how do we break away from the one and get into the other? Change is always difficult, but it is possible and rewarding. In this and subsequent chapters, you will re-

---

*For more on listening, agreeing, giving thanks, check the index.

ceive instructions to help you.*

Actually, you will probably discover that conversational prayer is the way you pray in your own heart, during the day, or in your own personal devotions.

For all prayer is a heart-language.

AN OUTLINE OF CONVERSATIONAL PRAYER**

There are four basic steps of conversational prayer which form an easily recalled framework. All of my work with groups and conferences and all of the teaching in this book are based on these four steps. The descriptive phrases that accompany each step in the outline below help us see what each involves and what is their Scriptural basis.

1. *Jesus is here.*   The power of worship
                         Realizing God's presence
                         Accepting God's love
                         Matthew 18:19, 20
2. *Thank you, Lord.*   The power of thanksgiving
                         Speaking from our hearts
                         Freedom from fear
                         Philippians 4:4-7
3. *Help me, Lord.*   The power of confession
                         Affirming one another
                         Receiving love
                         James 5:13-16
4. *Help my brother.*   The power of intercession
                         Giving away our love
                         Receiving answers
                         Mark 11:22-25

*Also check the index under Traditional.
**The four basic steps that follow are from Rosalind Rinker, *Communicating Love Through Prayer* (Grand Rapids: Zondervan Publishing House, 1966), pp. 95-96). Used by permission.

Notice the progression in the steps:
1. We start with our Lord and with worship.
2. Gratitude opens our hearts and our mouths.
3. We pray for ourselves and for those present.
4. We include those who are not present.

A DRAMATIZATION OF CONVERSATIONAL PRAYER

In the very brief, incomplete illustration given below, I have attempted a preview of dialogue prayer—how it begins to break barriers, promote reality, lift burdens, teach thankfulness, honesty, and brevity.

Prayer is the language of the heart, but too seldom do we listen or give expression to what it is saying. We do not need to beg or to plead when we pray, for our Lord is present. We only need courage to speak, belief in his love for us, and faith to claim his promise which is recorded in Matthew 18:19, 20.

DIALOGUE PRAYER
Four persons: J., R., H., S.
Setting: A small group anywhere.
1. *Notice the prayer-subjects.*
   J. Thank you, Lord Jesus, for being here.
   R. Lord, we worship you from our hearts.
   H. Thank you, Lord, for my family.
   R. I thank you for *my* family.
   J. And for mine.
   S. I especially thank you for my friends (name them if you wish), *and* for my father and my mother.
2. *Prayer is personal.*
   J. Lord, we all need to be more faithful in our daily lives and in our witness. Help us to glorify your Name.

(*Question:* What was left out here? Try it again.)

J. Lord, forgive me that I am not a faithful witness. I need your help. Make me sensitive . . . to the people I work with every day . . . to my folks at home, too.

3. Prayer is response.

H. Lord, I agree with J.'s prayer.

S. Assure him of your forgiveness.

R. Remind him . . . daily . . . that you *are* giving him sensitivity for people.

J. Thank you for those prayers. And thank you, too, Lord, for the answer.

In order to enter fully into the spirit of this illustration, ask four persons to take the parts of Jay, Ray, Hal, and Sam (or make them feminine). Ask the four to stand in a semicircle before the group. Have a quiet moment for them to read the dramatization through silently with the prayer that each one will enter into the part fully. They shouldn't "play" it, but pray it, even though the lines are being read.

You should, of course, preface this role-playing by reading together the description and the outline in the first part of this chapter. Afterwards, ask the group, "What happened here?" Let the group react to your question. Then, if necessary, ask some of the following questions.

Evaluation

1. Locate the four basic steps in the prayers just given.

2. How soon did the group become personal? Who started it? What else do we find out about him in this illustration?

3. Compare the two prayers J. gave. Which one means more? Why? What difference does it make to the one who says it? to those who hear it?

4. What did H. do here?

He picked up J.'s prayer and agreed* with him, as Jesus taught us to do. This is prayer-response, which meets such an important need for us: giving support, belonging, approval, and assurance.

5. What did the others do?

They showed love (concern and interest) by mentioning some of the very things J. asked for.

They did not condemn him, nor give him examples, nor preach at him.

The faith of an "outsider" (that is a person outside of or other than himself) gives him a kind of absolution** which his faith can grasp, and assures him that God is answering his prayer.

6. What did this brief encounter in conversational prayer begin to accomplish or set in motion for these four? For the group listening? (Reread the two paragraphs that introduce this dramatization.)

7. Could your group try it "for real"? Stand in a circle, now, and try it for about two minutes.

More detailed instructions can be found for teaching a group (and you may prefer to use them) in Chapters 4 through 7.

This kind of prayer looks pretty simple on paper, but spoken by real persons— from the heart—the impact can be dynamic.

The simplicity of this dramatization may have done one of two things to you. It may have encouraged you to feel that conversational prayer is not as difficult as you thought it would be, and as a result you are eager to try it. Or, its very

---

*See index on Agreeing.
**See index on Prayer-response, Absolution.

simplicity may have dismayed you into thinking that this isn't what you want after all. If this was your reaction, the illustration fooled you, because hidden in that simplicity is the sharp edge of the Holy Spirit piercing our carefully shielded complacency and privacy.

This is how love is given and received in the context of conversational prayer. Revealing personal need breaks down barriers between people and removes masks. There is an immediate outgoingness. Anxiety and guilt are relieved. Someone cares.

This is dialogue prayer, with a sense of our Lord's presence to love us and to accept us.

CHAPTER REVIEW
(for the leader first—for the group later)

1. From the description of conversational prayer, find and list the differences between it and traditional prayer. (seven or more):

traditional prayer   *conversational prayer*

2. How does one show love to another person in prayer?

3. How does my thank-you-response give another's faith a boost and help him believe for the answer to his request?

4. What three ingredients make any communication meaningful including conversational prayer?

5. Do the dramatization. Then use the questions under Evaluation as a teaching device. Your group may come up with more answering ideas than the text contains.

SUPPLEMENTARY READING
for Chapter 2

Book and page   *Subject*

CONVERSATIONAL PRAYER DESCRIBED
I   pp. 24-26   To a campus group
II pp. 89-96 (ch. 11)   "Discovering Joy in Prayer"
                         (the four steps are also outlined)

CONVERSATIONAL PRAYER DRAMATIZED
I   pp. 25-28   By students
I   pp. 30-31   Using God's Name meaningfully
I   pp. 38-39   In a Manhattan coffee shop
II pp. 115-117   Praying for another in a group
II pp. 113-114   Admitting a failure

SOME RESULTS
I   pp. 36-39 (ch. 5)   "Beginning a New Relationship"
I   pp. 72-73   In an Illinois church
I   pp. 74-75   Dr. Parker's prayer experiment
III pp. 63-68 (ch. 7)   Benefits of praying together
III pp. 55-59   Answers
III pp. 79-85 (ch. 9)   Interdenominational discoveries
III pp. 93-95 (ch. 10) A changed life

Chapter 3

✤ ✤ ✤

EXPERIENCING
GOD'S LOVE AND PRESENCE

This chapter is an introduction to the first two steps of conversational prayer—*Jesus is here,* and *Thank you, Lord.*

Come with me to a group meeting where we experience God's love and presence. The words in italics are spoken audibly by the leader, or by the group together.

✤ ✤ ✤

For where two or three
are
gathered
together
in my name
THERE AM I
in the midst of them.

Hearing these words spoken audibly enables me to accept them mentally—and immediately, for me, Jesus is there, with us in the group.

We are in God's presence.
Jesus is here. Here with us. Here with us now.
My heart is expectant. My mind is at attention. My body becomes quiet and relaxed.

For all who will quietly but audibly make these simple statements of affirmation* together with reverence and attention, for all who are present,

Jesus is here!

This is the miracle . . . that He is here for all in this room, for we are gathered in His name.
We are not alone. Jesus is here with us.
We are at home.
We are loved—we are accepted—by Jesus Christ and by each other.

THE POWER OF AFFIRMATION

In my travels to many states, speaking in churches of many denominations during the past ten years, holding prayer workshops and introducing conversational prayer, I have witnessed this phenomenon again and again—that Jesus Christ becomes real to those present, and they experience his love and presence. There is no big secret other than that which you just read in the paragraphs above.

Within a period of a few moments the whole group (usually all strangers to me and many to each other) have experienced the presence of God with us—his presence within us and around us, imparting acceptance, understanding, comfort and love—a presence not of this world. It is God's presence which opens our hearts to him and to each other. Even our mouths are opened to express worship and thanksgiving—to attempt, if possible, to express the sudden overflow we are experiencing within.

---

*See index under Affirmation, Presence.

How does this happen?

We take the words of Jesus in Matthew 18:20 to be true and reliable and to be acted upon literally. In a manner unexplainable except for the Holy Spirit, we are able to believe that Jesus is here. We become conscious of our living Lord by focusing our attention upon him. The reality of his presence with us is experienced by all in the group.

You may think yourself to be one who has difficulty in "feeling" the sense of his presence. Actually, the word *feel* is not altogether correct. We are mentally aware, a state which borders on feeling, because we are focusing attention on Jesus' words. This "feeling" is attention with concentration. If you don't "feel" anything or are not mentally aware of anything, affirm the words anyway by repeating them: *Jesus is here*. The words are true—he *is* here. Later, in all probability, you'll be aware of his presence as the rest of us are. This is the power of affirmation.

THE PROMISE TO THE SMALL GROUP

What did we do to experience the presence of Jesus?

Nothing which you cannot do. In fact, as I go on through these pages I will have shared with you most of the ways by which I teach others.

Here is an unexpected development which has come to me personally. I have finally realized that I am more aware of the risen Lord Jesus—and his love and presence—when I am with a group, whether of friends or of strangers, than when I am alone in my own room. At first I was slow to admit this, as though something must be wrong with me for having such an idea. But as this experience was repeated, I humbly accepted it and finally was able to speak of it authentically.

New situations bring new ideas to me—guidance from the

Spirit, I call them. This is not spiritualism or hypnotism; it is centered on Jesus Christ and he is the only one to whom I surrender myself, my mind, and my thoughts. I am convinced that if we are to be teachers of prayer, we must share these intimate experiences.

Recently I read this statement by Ben Johnson of the Department of Lay Evangelism in the Southern Methodist Church: "We become most aware of His presence in the fellowship of the small group." This man, through his extensive travels and constant meeting with groups has found and acknowledged the same experience.

Is it so unbelievable for us to take the words of Jesus and act on them? To say those words and believe them? To expect the promised result?

> For where two or three
> are gathered in my name
> there am I.

THE PRESENCE OF JESUS

In Chapters 4 and 5 of this book you will be reading and practicing dry-run instructions for leading a small group through Steps I and II of conversational prayer. These instructions are deceptively simple, yet they are, in fact, almost the very words I use when I teach a new group to pray conversationally.

Just as important as the words, however, are the accompanying actions: we stand up, hold hands, form a circle . . . and with closed eyes in a quiet attitude of prayer, we listen together to the words of Jesus in the promise quoted at the beginning of this chapter.

Here we have touch. We feel another's hand warmly in ours. We have comfort and a certain security. We stand for maximum attention. Our eyes are closed to shut out all else. We have concentration. The words we hear following the words of Jesus suggest to us what we have been longing to hear. Their disarming simplicity and brevity is immediately seized upon by our hearts without hesitation and without argument.

We are there. And Jesus is there. And suddenly nobody else seems to matter. He and I are alone. And I am able to be near him. Does he touch me . . . or do I touch him? It doesn't matter. I am comforted. I am known. I am accepted without question and without reservation. My soul is restored. I am quieted and weaned from my adult fear of rejection. I belong.

All this takes place within a few short seconds of time. Each time I experience more, and that is added to what I have already felt. But what I experience is real to me. In a moment, when we open our eyes, drop hands, and look with tentative reservations into the eyes of others in that circle, I see mirrored there what I myself have just experienced.

Do we talk about it?

Sometimes yes and sometimes no. One may put it this way. "We were all strangers when we went into that circle, except for short introductions. After those first few moments of worship in the presence of our Lord, we were not strangers any more. We loved one another. We were all caught up in the miracle of being with Jesus."

After such an experience at a women's retreat with about 25 present, I asked, "Would anyone like to talk about what happened?" There they sat, looking at me. I stood very relaxed and smiled at them, not really expecting anyone to say anything; I only wanted them to think again about what they had experienced.

Suddenly a woman spoke, "I would. The little girl within me just got up and went over to where Jesus was, and I put my head against his arm and started to cry. He put his arms around me, and I felt better . . ." She stopped, suddenly shy. "That's all I remember."

Then, one after the other, five or six shared their experience of that brief moment. How real it was to each one of them! The shining eye, the tear brushed away, gave evidence that the remembrance of that brief encounter was to remain always a special treasure no one could snatch away. We sat there, not saying more, thinking of what had been said, of unspoken things within our own hearts—yet drawn very close together in the union and unity which Jesus said would be given to those who believe upon his name (John 17:11, 26).

QUESTION:
Why don't we have more such experiences?
ANSWER:
Well, why don't we? You can answer that as well as I can. In this materialistic, intellectual world of ours, we play at "following the leader," and what is important to him finally becomes the *norm* and the accepted procedure for the rest of us. We are afraid of being different, of change, of being ourselves, of worship from our inmost hearts, of being children together in God's presence.

QUESTION:
You would like to be in one of my circles and experience this? I think I heard you say that.
ANSWER:
Why not have a circle of your own? God is no respecter of persons. What I have discovered, I write about in order that others, including you, may experience it also.

Whom having not seen, ye love.—*I Peter 1:8.*
Love one another, as I have loved you. This is my commandment.—*John 15:12.*

CHAPTER REVIEW*

1. Since action precedes feeling, answer this question by listing the actions that are aids to mental stimulation: How does one become aware of the presence of our risen Lord? (A possible seven or more.)

2. What are the results of experiencing the presence of Jesus Christ?

these negatives go   *these positives come*

3. What single words express what has been experienced? Or ask the question this way: Using the following words, explain how they characterize a group experience of "being as little children" in the presence of Jesus.

togetherness	awareness	affirmation
unity	concentration	simplicity
worship	expectancy	joy

---

*NOTE *to teacher:* The exercises in this chapter review may need to wait until after Steps I and II (Chapters 4 and 5) have been taught. You may use them at any later date with the group, but work them out for yourself *now*.

MEDITATION EXERCISE

1. Prepare a meditation on being with Jesus. (If you have Book II, meditations appear on pages 35, 42, 49, 104.) Do this by marking sentences or phrases from this chapter which are suitable. Include some of your own thoughts of worship as connecting links. See also the meditation on God's love at the end of Chapter 4 (reprinted from Book II).

2. Use the meditations prepared by group members in future meetings as an introduction to the prayer time. Let one person read quietly while the others give their concentrated attention.

3. How does such a meditation answer these questions:

a. What do people do with feelings of aloneness, rejection, bitterness, depression?

b. How can the meditation help break these attitudes down?

c. What can we do to reeducate ourselves and each other?

d. What negative conditioning have people been exposed to?

e. Define positive conditioning.

Important: Be children together in God's presence.

SUPPLEMENTARY READING
for Chapter 3

All of Book II is on this subject, but see especially the first
five chapters, and the meditations on pp. 35, 42, 49, 104.
For assistance in reeducating negative feelings about God's
love to positive ones (that is, to answer the question, "Does
God love me?), your group will want to listen to my record,
God Loves You, W-6152-LP, Word Records, Waco, Texas.

Book and page	Subject
II pp. 60-65, 90	Being childlike
I p. 31	Praying to Jesus Christ
I pp. 51-53	Worship
I pp. 95-111	"Aids to Personal Worship"
II pp. 81-88 (ch. 10)	"God's Kind of Love"
III pp. 39-44 (ch. 4)	"A Meeting Where Love Is Expressed"

PART TWO

✛ ✛ ✛

Teaching
The Four
Basic Steps

Introduction to Chapters 4 & 5

✤ ✤ ✤

General Lesson Plan
for Steps I & II

This lesson plan covers the first two basic steps of conversational prayer—*Jesus is here,* and *Thank you, Lord.*

1. *As leader,* you will, of course, have read all the preceding chapters. You will also find it helpful to check the index for subjects which apply to you and to your group at this time.

2. If you are teaching *a new group,* you need also to have read Book I.

3. *At your first meeting:*

a) Explain the differences between monologue and dialogue prayer, the benefits of conversational prayer,* and the four steps of prayer, merely mentioning Steps III and IV since they come later.

b) Give the group some inspirational material—read a portion from this book to motivate them (from Chapter 3); have someone share what conversational prayer has already meant to them; or try the dramatization given in Chapter 2.

4. Having done your homework on Chapters 4 and 5, take

your group right into the dry-run outlines of Step I and Step II, and experience them together.

5. Group evaluation for this first session will be found at the close of Chapter 5.

---

*Check the index on these subjects.

Chapter 4

✤ ✤ ✤

STEP I—JESUS IS HERE
THE POWER OF WORSHIP

The previous chapter introduced you to the first step of prayer—*Jesus is here*—and to the transforming power of experiencing Jesus' presence in worship. In imagination we have heard the presence of Jesus affirmed; we have responded with our own affirmations, and have experienced his love removing our fears and doubts.

THE VALUE OF DRY-RUN OUTLINES

Some of you who are enthusiastic, natural teachers could go right into a group with no more help than Chapters 1 through 3 and lead the members into this kind of transforming prayer. Most of us, however, need more step-by step guidance. And that is what I will give you in the next four chapters.

This step-by-step guidance is in the form of what I call

"dry-run outlines." Although I have provided them primarily for beginners with little or no experience in audible praying, everyone will find them helpful. They will give you the actual words to say when you begin to teach the group, and are to be practiced thoroughly ahead of time—there are to be plenty of dry runs! These outlines have proven to be valuable teaching aids. They work! You will find, too, that they will provide the inspiration and encouragement the group needs.

Before you go any further, turn back to Chapter 2 and review the four basic steps of conversational prayer. Steps I and II—*Jesus is here,* and *Thank you, Lord*—belong together, as do Steps III and IV. Although I have devoted a separate chapter to each step, the first two steps should be presented to your group in a single session. (They may, of course, be used separately at your discretion.)

The first two steps are very brief and simple. Both can be experienced in ten minutes by a group of beginners (that time does not include the explanatory and inspirational material which is presented first). Or they may occupy the best part of an hour as old-timers pray together.

As you follow the instructions in the dry-run outline, may I alert you to two important things:
1. The use of silence.* Silence enables us to learn quietness within and to sense the presence of our Lord.
2. The use of tonal qualities in your voice as leader when you give instructions.

Make both these things subjects for prayer. God will help you to be aware and sensitive to the needs of the persons in your group. Your voice is a means of touching them—like invisible but tangible hands.

---

*Check index under Silence.

DIRECTIONS FOR USING THE DRY-RUN OUTLINES

Remember: conversational prayer is a free form of dialogue prayer between people who are moving in acceptance toward one another because of the love of Christ.

✠ ✠ ✠

1. Priority must be given to the first step of prayer—the presence of Jesus—because of its vital importance in the spiritual life of the individual as well as of the group. Never underestimate the dynamic power of this first step. Don't forget, however, that Steps I and II should be presented together. So go on to the dry-run outline in Chapter 5 when you have worked through the one in this chapter.

2. For receiving your first impressions and trying to identify with your group, read the Procedure with a piece of paper covering the Purpose. Try to visualize your group. Try to be a member of that group as though you were being taught how to pray.

3. Now, start again and read both Procedure and Purpose as they are written, side by side. Pray for a quiet mind to understand both *what* you are doing and *why* you are doing it.

4. When you are ready, test yourself. Cover the Purpose side. Are you able to state the purpose in your own words? Do you follow the progression, the *why* of each part? Study and practice the Procedure side aloud until you are sure of each part and its relation to the steps which precede and follow.

5. Do your practicing audibly. You will find these ideas being firmly implanted in your mind. The exact words are not important. Make a brief word-outline of your own to guide you.

6. Pray conversationally with a friend or two using this outline, until (it will happen quite suddenly sometimes) you've gone beyond the method to the very spirit of it all. If

you leave out or add a word or an idea here and there, that's fine. You may even wish to reverse the order of the four steps. Let the creativity flow.

7. Your own knowledge of these concepts will project itself to your hearers. If you do not grasp the true significance, neither will they. Be prepared for cooperation from them. They may surprise you and be a step ahead of you much of the time. Or, they may spontaneously introduce something new and wonderful. We are all taught by the same Spirit when our hearts are open.

8. Remember: You are not teaching a lesson. You are teaching people to pray.

"They who gave the world the Book of Psalms have been a people of prayer. This the rabbis define as worship by the heart. It is not so much petition as it is the bringing of man into harmony with the universal spirit by attuning the soul to communion with God."

—David de Sola Pool, *Why I Am a Jew**

*Boston: Beacon Press, 1957, p. 92.

DRY-RUN OUTLINE

STEP I
JESUS IS HERE

The goal to keep in mind: Realizing the presence of God
by a directed meditation.

Notes for the leader:
1. Suggested pauses for silence and comparative lengths
   are indicated by one or more of this sign ⸕.
2. Any directive remarks to you under Procedure will be
   in parentheses.
3. Everything else under Procedure may be said directly to
   the group.

Procedure

(how)

Purpose

(why)

1. Let's stand and make a circle of love. (Do it.)

1. Prayer is easier for beginners when they are on
their feet. They think "This
can't last too long if we're
standing."

2. Shall we take hands? ⸕ The
circle symbolizes our invisible
union with Christ.

2. Physical contact is non-
verbal communication. Our
need for tangible warmth of
feeling and touch must be
reemphasized.

3. This is our silent worship
time. ⸕ ⸕ ⸕

3. Hearing this further re-
laxes them. They will not
be expected to pray audi-
bly.

4. Let's take an attitude of prayer. You don't need to close your eyes, but if you do, you'll find you can concentrate better. ⸜ ⸜

4. You are teaching them a new kind of prayer-meditation, so don't hurry. Have these ideas well in mind.

5. Now, I'd like your *full* attention for about two minutes. By an act of your will, put out of your mind ⸜ all that happened before you came here— ⸜ ⸜ all that will happen after you leave here. ⸜ ⸜

5. As you say this, they will be doing it. Your words will carry belief. Watch the tone of your voice—make it steady and not high. When you tell them they *can* do it, they *are* doing it.

6. Hear the words of Jesus. ⸜ ⸜ ⸜ Again I say to you, ⸜ if two of you agree on earth about anything they ask, ⸜ it will be done for them by my Father in heaven. For where two or three are gathered in my name ⸜ *there am I* ⸜ ⸜ ⸜ in the midst of them. ⸜ ⸜

6. Matt. 18:19, 20 RSV (or any version you like). Let the tone of your voice convey the meaning. Say words distinctly. Practice aloud many times alone. Your voice may be the key to participation for someone present. Listening is also prayer.

7. *Jesus* is here. Jesus ⸜ is in our midst. ⸜ Think what he would be like ⸜ if you could actually see him, ⸜ welcome him, ⸜ ⸜ worship him. ⸜ ⸜

7. You do not need to announce silence; just let the pauses come. They will learn to appreciate silence and to enjoy it—a little at a time. Silence is also prayer.

8. Visualize Jesus ⸜ if you can. Do you have a favorite picture? Or a church window you remember? I like to look at his hands and his feet— ⸜ ⸜ the marks of love are there. ⸜ ⸜

8. Some people object to pictures of Jesus, so I use all these ideas. Mental concentration is also prayer.

9. Be a little child, ⸕ ⸕ now, ⸕ in Jesus' presence, ⸕ and worship him. ⸕ ⸕ ⸕

9. People's attention span is very short; give them a few seconds. You, too, be a child . . . and worship.

10. Jesus *is* here. ⸕ ⸕ *Jesus* is here. ⸕ ⸕ Jesus is *here.* ⸕ ⸕ (The wonder of it!)

10. More worship. You may have enough material, and wish to use this as an alternate for #8 next time. Don't be afraid to let the worship of your heart reveal itself through your voice. Be real.

11. Jesus is saying to you: "My child, I *love* you. ⸕ I know all about you." ⸕ He is saying, "My child, I *accept* you just as you are. ⸕ My child, I *care* about *you.* ⸕ My child, I *forgive* you."* ⸕ ⸕

11. Worship becomes personal now. Sensing Christ with us enables us to speak with him later. For now, just sense his nearness. Emphasize the verbs here.

12. I'm going to repeat the four ways God loves you, so that you may repeat them silently in your heart with me. "My child, I love you. ⸕ My child, I accept you. ⸕ My child, I care about you. ⸕ My child, I forgive you. ⸕ Because, you see, I love you."* ⸕

12. These are very important truths, not only for prayer, but for living. They are *affirmations* of love, faith, and assurance, and grow in depth with repetition. As you say them, your group will be affirming them from within their hearts. Whether they know it or not, this too is prayer.

---

*For the complete meditation, see Chapter 4, p. 52. It is also available in card form from the author at $2.00 per hundred. A card giving the four basic steps of conversational prayer is also available at the same price.

CLOSING

(Optional—omit if you go right into Step II with no explanations)

13. Lord Jesus, ┐ we give thanks to you for being with us, ┐ for loving each one of us, ┐ accepting us just as we are. ┐ We worship you, ┐ now and forever. ┐ ┐ Amen. ┐

13. Always, the leader closes the prayer time by a very simple sentence, speaking for the whole group by the pronoun *we*.

14. Let's drop hands and take a break as I explain Step II. (Read the Scripture and goals from the beginning of Chapter 5, and then go right into #1 of the Dry-run for Step II.)

14. Standing keeps attention concentrated and makes verbal participation easier. They can sit at the end of the next lesson.

✠ ✠ ✠

Time: These 14 steps will take about three minutes when you practice alone. If you use less time, slow up at each ┐ or at commas. People need time to think, to visualize—but not too much time at first. You will use more than three minutes when you are with the group.

CHAPTER REVIEW
(for the leader first—for the group later)

1. *What do these qualities*
                              or ideas   *do for us?*
learning to be silent
use of voice control
knowing the subject matter
standing to pray
awareness of feelings
sense of touch: hands
symbol of the circle
power of silent worship
thought control
listening
creative imagination
childlikeness
"Jesus is here"
affirmations of love

2. What carryover could these qualities have for us in daily life?

Suggestion: Select one this week to practice or meditate on, and note the result in attitude or actions. This exercise would provide excellent *thank-you* material for opening sessions as you proceed into Step II.

MEDITATION

1. *My child, I love you.*
   I love you unconditionally.
   I love you, good or bad, with no strings attached.
   I love you like this because I know all about you.
   I have known you ever since you were a child.
   I know what I can do for you.
   I know what I want to do for you.
2. *My child, I accept you.*
   I accept you just as you are.
   You don't need to change yourself.
   I'll do the changing when you are ready.
   I love you just as you are.
   Believe this—for I assure you it is true.
3. *My child, I care about you.*
   I care about every big or little thing which happens to you.
      Believe this.
   I care enough to do something about it. Remember this.
   I will help you when you need me. Ask me.
   I love you.
   I accept you.
   I care about you.
4. *My child, I forgive you.*
   I forgive you, and my forgiveness is complete.
   It is not like that of humans who forgive but cannot forget.
   I love you. My arms are open with love.
   Please come here! Come here to me!
   I forgive you.
   I carried it all for you on the cross.
   Believe this. It is true.
   REJOICE . . . AND BE GLAD

*From *Communicating Love Through Prayer* (Grand Rapids: Zondervan Publishing House, 1966), p. 104. Used by permission.

SUPPLEMENTARY READING
for Chapter 4

Book and page	*Subject*
I pp. 41-42, 47	He promises it
I p. 48	He is here (summary)
I p. 112 (or p. 33)	Diagram of the Trinity
I pp. 24-39	What do I believe about Jesus
(chs. 3-5)	Christ?
II pp. 99-104 (ch. 4)	"The Presence of God"

Chapter 5

✤ ✤ ✤

STEP II—THANK YOU, LORD
THE POWER OF THANKSGIVING

REJOICE EVERMORE. I Thessalonians 5:16

Thanksgiving has the power to open hearts.
Thanksgiving has the power to join hearts.
Praise and thanksgiving have the power to wash away the bitterness of life.
Praise and thanksgiving are restorers of youth.
Praise and thanksgiving are removers of mountains.

"As you learn to thank Me more and more, you will more and more see Me in the little happenings of daily life, and increasingly see much about which to rejoice."*

"Delight yourselves in the Lord;
yes, find your joy in him at all times.

---

*From *God at Eventide,* A. J. Russell, ed. (New York: Dodd, Mead & Co., 1950), p. 164.

Have a reputation for gentleness,
and never forget the nearness of your Lord.
Don't worry over anything whatever;
tell God every detail of your needs
in earnest and thankful prayer,
and the peace of God,
which transcends human understanding,
will keep constant guard
over your hearts and minds
as they rest in Christ Jesus."*

"In Jewish tradition prayer becomes a joyous spiritual exercise. It is essentially the expression of thanksgiving for the privileges of life."**

---

*Philippians 4:4-7 from J. B. Phillips, *The New Testament in Modern English.*
**de Sola Pool, *op. cit.,* p. 92.

DRY-RUN OUTLINE

STEP II
THANK YOU, LORD

Goals to keep in mind: Freedom from fear of audible prayer.
Speaking when our hearts prompt us.

Procedure

1. Giving thanks is a way to worship God, too. I will be directing you, so please relax. Freedom is one of our goals . . . here's one way to get it.

2. (Smile expectantly.) How many of you find audible prayer difficult? (Expect reactions.) Look at the hands! (Commend and encourage.) Any more?

3. Let's take hands again and make our circle of love. Our second step is, *Thank you, Lord.*

4. Our first audible thank-you is to be for each other. Be sure you know the first name of the person on either side of you. (Wait until they do.)

Purpose

1. Remember these are instructions for a first-time group. They may be tense and uneasy.

2. Lift your own hand as you ask that question and admit, "That includes me." Several brave ones will lift theirs, and then more will also. Laughter usually follows as people relax.

3. This reestablishes us as a belonging-group. The sense of touch reassures us personally. This next part is apt to be difficult for some.

4. Some in the group are not quite ready to pray aloud, and so we will go around the circle this once, but *never* again. We want to develop the freedom to speak when the spirit moves us.

5. Now, let us go around the circle, giving thanks for the persons on either side of us. Look right into his eyes and say, *Thank you, Lord, for Larry.* He does the same to you, using your name, then turns to the person on the other side of him, and so on. I'll start, you follow. (You will start, and you may also be the last person to express thanks. There may be a little loving confusion, but that's all right.)

5. This is a real blockbuster and it works. The sound-barrier is broken for many as they hear their own voice saying something meaningful in the context of prayer. We *can* pray with our eyes open.

Appreciation is a form of giving thanks.

6. Now, in this next part, don't try to think up something to say. If your heart starts pounding, you're the next one to pray —and the words will be there. If someone says your prayer . . . go ahead and say it anyhow. That makes it really yours. If all of us should repeat the same thing, that's great. That's love in action.

6. You are teaching them now, on their feet, and they are listening. You are relieving them of fear—of their own voices, of saying something the wrong way, of comparison. You are teaching the value of repetition in prayer.

7. Eyes closed now ✔ ✔ for concentration while I read to you. (Read Philippians 4: 4-7.)

7. Listening with eyes closed does help one to concentrate.

8. Remember, ✔ Jesus is here. ✔ ✔ Let's give him our full attention ✔ ✔ and open our hearts to him. ✔ ✔ ✔

8. Be quiet. The short silences will become more meaningful as time goes on.

9. We're going to give thanks by remembering the four ways Jesus loves us. One of them has a special meaning for you. Let's repeat them aloud together:
My child, I love you.
My child, I accept you.
My child, I care about you.
My child, I forgive you.

9. They learned these a few moments ago in Step I, and also as they gave non-verbal thanks in their hearts. Now . . . you are helping them to be vocal.

10. Remember, when your heart starts to beat rapidly, it's your turn.

10. This is especially helpful for those who find audible prayer difficult . . . for one who has never prayed aloud.

11. I'll start, then you say yours, no matter how many times it has been said. *"Thank you, Lord Jesus, for loving me."*

11. As you start, they will follow. Insist on just one sentence chosen from the four preferably (although it doesn't matter). No closing amens.

12. (When you feel it is time, move on to:) Now let's give thanks for other *things* or for *people* in our lives. Keep it short—one sentence. Mention first names only. (You start.)

12. Watch for the traditional pray-er who gives thanks for three or four things. Gently teach by saying, "Thank you, John, for that prayer, but we want to limit ourselves to just *one* thank-you for now." He'll get the point. And the shy ones will feel freer to speak up.

13. (Where needed, use this:) Remember, say your thank-you, even if someone else said it. It's yours. Repetition is a part of true worship.

13. Repetition is the secret of good teaching. Teach it by example, too. When one gives thanks, you say, "Yes, Lord, I thank you too" . . . or "Lets all say 'Thank you Lord' on that one . . ." and they will, with relief.

14. (When closing use this:) Thank you, Lord Jesus, for all these prayers, and for the ones still in our hearts. Amen.

14. Close with a simple prayer like this . . . unless you have decided to go right into Steps III & IV. If this is your first, very first, time, *take a break*.

Time: from six to eight minutes.

15. What do we do next? We take a break.

15. *Sit down and talk* about what you did. You may check the index for evaluation helps, but for right now, use the suggestions that follow. Give people time to speak up.

GROUP EVALUATION
for Steps I & II

1. If you only taught Steps I and II (leaving III & IV until next time as suggested) use this evaluation. Don't expect too much participation from your group now. They will have more reactions to share after you give them the next steps—

that is, after you have done all four steps at one time.

2. *Tell the group:*

You have had your first lesson in conversational prayer. When God is far away, prayer is difficult. Prayer is simplified when Jesus is near us, with us, and within us. This first lesson is very important. *Each* time we pray together we should include it—even if we merely pause to recognize him and to say, "Thank you, Lord Jesus, for being here."

3. *Ask for discussion:*

a) Let's talk about some of the things we just did in our prayer time. Name a few.

b) (After some participation, ask:) What did you particularly like about this kind of praying? (Or:) What did you personally like the best?

4. As you listen to their reactions, you may mentally pinpoint what they learned and what still needs to be taught. Remember that people have a tendency not to tell everything in public. Many will come to you later and share something wonderful from this session.

5. *Plan for your second meeting.*

a) With the group, agree on a time and a place.

b) As leader, plan to start each time with Steps I and II. You need to keep on repeating this part of the prayer time until any one of the group can lead it in your place. In your second meeting go right on from this first part into Steps III and IV without a break. In all your meetings after that, always use all four steps or parts of them.

6. Remember: Discussion and evaluation are always part of learning. Use the suggestions from #3 above next time, or try the chapter review that follows. Or try your own questions.

7. Now you are on your way!

Freedom is an experience, not a theory.

CHAPTER REVIEW
(for the leader first—for the group later)

What do the following actions
                    or ideas   do for us?

thanksgiving
freedom
giving audible thanks
touching
listening
value of repetition
release from fear
personally loved
personally accepted
short thank-you's
(add others to this list)

SUPPLEMENTARY READING
for Chapter 5

Book and Page	*Subject*
I pp. 40-47 (ch. 6)	"Why Pray Aloud Together?"
II pp. 105-110 (ch. 13)	"The Power of Gratitude"
II pp. 121-124	Thanking before receiving
III p. 57	The gift of a thankful spirit
III p. 59	Setting apart time for thanksgiving

You might also want to read the chapter "The Thankful Heart" in my book *The Open Heart* (formerly *Becoming a Christian*), published by Zondervan Publishing House.

Introduction to Chapters 6 & 7

✤ ✤ ✤

General Lesson Plan
for Steps III & IV

1. To introduce Step III (Help me, Lord) to a new group, use the Scripture and the invitation to confession from Chapter 6. Before you read these to them, ask the group to listen with alertness since you will quiz them afterwards. This will prepare them for the "rules of the game" in knowing what to admit and what not to admit.

2. Introduce Step IV (Help my brother) at the same time by using these pointers:

 a) "When the time comes, we will go right into Step IV without a break. I'll instruct you. The difference is that while we pray for persons present in Step III, we pray for persons not present in Step IV."

 b) *How:* Go right from #16 of the dry-run outline in Chapter 6 to #1 of Chapter 7. You will be using the "Prayer of Love." Study that section in Chapter 7 for further preparation.

3. *Dry-run outlines:* a practical word here. Try handling them on a subject (or single word to remind you) basis first.

Make your own outline. Don't try to get every single thing into the prayer time the first or second session. Work on that gradually, and each time you'll be able to add more—until you'll even branch out on your own and ad lib as the Spirit leads you.

4. If you are leading a more advanced group, you would do well to follow the same instructions the first few times. After the pattern is set (learned) the variations come naturally. You may wish to use Step IV before you use Step III.

5. For various reasons Step III—*Help me, Lord*—is the one most frequently omitted from the prayer time. Perhaps the real reason for its omission is that it is the most difficult prayer to pray. It is not easy to expose oneself. But do include it. Give the group a chance. Give yourself a chance. Give God a chance.

Remember: The necessary courage to be honest in a group is found in God's acceptance and in each other's acceptance. We continually need to remind ourselves of
the unconditional love
of Jesus Christ
who accepts me just as I am because
he knows just what he can do for me.

And the love of God
brought into action
by our very weakness,
will unite us
to his strength.

Chapter 6

❖ ❖ ❖

STEP III—HELP ME, LORD
THE POWER OF CONFESSION

If we confess our sins, he is faithful and just to forgive us our sins, and to cleanse us from all unrighteousness.

—*I John 1:9*

❖ ❖ ❖

Is there any one of you who is in trouble? He should pray. . . . Is there any one of you who is sick? He should call the church elders, who will pray for him and pour oil on him in the name of the Lord. This prayer, made in faith, will save the sick man. . . .*

You should get into the habit of admitting your sins to one another, and praying for one another, so that if sickness comes to you, you may be healed. . . .**

The prayer of a righteous man has a powerful effect.*

—*James 5:13-16*

---

*James 5:13-16, *Good News for Modern Man,* copyright 1966 American Bible Society.
**James 5:16, Phillips.

INVITATION TO CONFESSION

Jesus is here!
End your loneliness.
Dare to join the fellowship
of sinners without their masks.

Tell him who you are,
not what you ought to be.
For most of us,
repentance comes afterwards,
not before.

Lay your cards on the table.
Call them by name if you can.
Tell as much as you can,
but be as brief as you can.
Tell your faults, not another's.
Pray in the first person—
say "I" when you mean *I,*
and "we" when all can be included.
Don't excuse or rationalize . . .
or pile up all the details.
Jesus knows, and he's here.
Ask and receive his forgiveness
and our affirmation.

Here we are, you and I—brothers—
what will we do?
We have a choice:
to fail our brother
by not listening,
by thinking of ourselves,
by not being quick to accept him;
or to touch him with affirmation
as love goes into action.

Because . . . he is wounded
. . . with an act to be forgiven,
. . . with a memory to be healed.

Jesus,
touch him with our words.
Jesus,
touch him with our hands.
In expectancy
and with thanksgiving,
Amen and Amen.

Sin is more than a lack of personal piety.
Sin is—failure to be in league with God's purpose.
　　　—withholding love from others.

DRY-RUN OUTLINE

STEP **III**
HELP ME, LORD!

Goals to keep in mind (with love):
>   To provide an opportunity for honesty.
>   To give affirmation, response, and absolution.
>   To experience forgiveness and to be forgiving.

✠   ✠   ✠

Notes for the leader:

In this column, you will find *your* lines, unless preceded by names like *Jane* or *Ted*. Instructions not be be said aloud are in parenthesis. At this sign ⸗ pause, with longer pauses for two and three signs. Learn to make your own pauses.

This column tells the reason why we do what we do in the other column. We are reminded of lessons to be learned. We are given material for answering questions after our prayer-time.

✠   ✠   ✠

Procedure

1. Now we are ready for Step III, where we bring our personal needs, our failures, our hang-ups to Jesus. We have received his love and acceptance. ⸗ Jesus is here to answer. ⸗ If you could see him, what would you like to ask him to do for you? ⸗ ⸗ ⸗

Purpose

1. You may give the group the goals, or write them on a blackboard. Give them a quiet second to think about that question. You'll repeat it again, soon.

2. Shall we link arms as we stand—for comfort, warmth, and support—and take an attitude of prayer?

2. Physical touch does give support and confidence to most persons, as they will soon discover. This is particularly needed for Step III.

3. What do you want Jesus to do for you? ✓ ✓ ✓ Ask him now ✓ silently. ✓ ✓ ✓ Admit your fault. ✓ ✓ Tell him your hang-up, not somebody else's. ✓ ✓ Tell him what's wrong. ✓ ✓ ✓

3. Some sins need silence. Others need only one listener. Some can and should be openly admitted to the group—for support in asking for forgiveness, for the affirmation that forgiveness has been granted, and for mutual acceptance in love. Give them plenty of time here for silent confession.

4. (You pray:) Thank you, Jesus, for hearing each one of us, and for forgiving each one of us. ✓ ✓ Let's say: *Thank you, Jesus,* together. (Say it.)

4. Continual giving of thanks is a prayer habit sometimes called *affirmation.* We affirm our gift (and another's) by saying *thank you.*

5. (You may wish to read once more part of "Invitation to Confession" or to repeat a Scripture verse. From now on, expect someone to break through and pray for himself. Give people a chance. Pause a moment, and silently love them all. You may not need all of #'s 6, 7, or 8, but do not be afraid of silence. Do not try to fill silence with more words. People heard. They struggle to speak. Wait for them . . . with love. Pour love on them as you wait. They'll get the message.)

6. Jesus is here. He accepts you. ✓ ✓ He knows all about you. ✓ Ask him for the help you need. ✓

6. Your voice in reading or speaking will help open, or close, the door—such a delicate balance. Be kind.

7. What do you want Jesus to do for you? ⟋ ⟋ Ask him.

7. Remember their shyness, fear, and inexperience. Help them.

8. (You pray first.) Lord, this is me, Ros (use your first name). I admit I'm half-afraid right now of my own inadequacy to teach something different. Forgive me. (Wait.) Thank you, Jesus, I trust you. ⟋ ⟋

8. Make it real, whatever you ask for. If no one gives a response (*says thank you*) give it yourself, after a brief pause. (See *Chapter 2, page 22,* for three ideas to keep in mind and to begin to practice in future sessions, if not in this one.)

(Example of what could happen:) 9. *Ted:* Lord, help me . . . there's this guy . . . at work . . . I hate his guts . . . forgive me.

9. You take this at once and affirm his request. Any revealing of the heart must have immediate prayer-response. Use his name.

10. Thank you, Lord, you do forgive Ted, right now. ⟋ ⟋ Ted, take it now—receive God's forgiveness. ⟋ ⟋ ⟋ Let's all say with Ted, *Thank you, Lord, for your forgiveness.*

10. Ted is included, is relieved at being able to speak out, and to give thanks immediately. The combined faith of the group aids in giving him both absolution and assurance.

11. *John:* Lord, I'd like to pray for that guy Ted works with. Give Ted your kind of caring about him now; he's probably got some hang-up of his own.

11. This is "keeping in tune." Encourage the group to pray in unison: *Thank you for answering that prayer.* This teaches expectation and affirmation— claiming Christ's promise that when at least two agree on a request, it will be done (Matt. 18:19).

12. Who else has something to ask? (Give them a fresh chance.)

12. Say it again. They always need an invitation.

13. *Jane:* Lord, this is me, Jane. I'm so impatient with my mother . . . forgive me (tears). (You) Will someone pray for Jane?

13. You can be sure that everyone is identifying with her, and feeling for her. One open heart gives courage to others. When there are tears, just say, "Tears are liquid love, God's safety valve for which we are grateful." This quickly ends any embarrassment.

14. *Lois* responds: Thank You, Lord, for forgiving Janie. (Then others, one after the other, pray for themselves or each other.)

14. Pick up their very words (as in indirect counseling) and use them in giving prayer-response, absolution or affirmation. Don't preach. Make it short. Give love that heals.

15. (Altogether.) *Thank you, Lord.*

15. They will learn to do this without your prompting.

16. (Cut it here.) Now we'll pray for persons not present, which is Step IV. We can always come back and pray for ourselves at any time. (See Chapter 7:1.)

16. Don't go on too long—then they'll be eager for the next meeting and ready for more.

The greatest joy may come later, after the meeting is over, perhaps on the way home. Suddenly a fresh sense of God's love and forgiveness, or the love of those in the group, will warm one through and through.

Love for one's brother
   is being willing to admit my failure rather than to keep silent
and imply that all is well when everything is wrong.

Personal difficulties
   are due not to the unconscious but to the unuttered.

THE VALUE OF TEARS

Tears are a gift from God. They act as a safety-valve for
our pent-up emotions. Be quick to offer your brother positive
help when his tears flow: "Thank you, Lord, for those tears—
for the healing going on right now."

When a person cannot continue an audible prayer because
of tears, someone in the group should offer a short prayer
like the one above. Then let several pray for that person and
for his request. In a very short time, he will have recovered
and will want to continue his prayer. He may even be ready
at that time to give thanks. Join him.

I have seen tears from one person open the hearts of every
person in that group to love one another. I have seen tears
shed by one brother set the whole group free to make the
requests they had been holding back on.

In an extreme case, where someone breaks into heavy un-
controlled sobbing, the act of love is for a concerned person
to take this person quietly away from the group until recovery
is possible. This may be the opportunity for loving prayer and
counseling which the group could not give.

LEADER'S PRE-CLASS AFFIRMATIONS OF FAITH

You have carefully prepared your lesson, and made your own outline. You have prayed for each member of your group. Relax now and trust God who is far more interested in growth and results than you are. Use these affirmations to focus your vision and your faith—pray them out loud.

Lord, I believe . . .

• that the members of the group will experience Christ's presence during conversational prayer, and will find their daily lives enriched by him.

• that the Holy Spirit will give to each one of us a spirit of praise and thanksgiving which will renew, unite, and ignite our faith as we move on to pray for ourselves and others.

• that each person will take part in asking for himself, and in responding to another.

• that this group will learn to pray together.

• that my presentation will be clear.

In the name of the Father,
and of the Son,
and of the Holy Ghost. AMEN.

LEADER'S AFTER-CLASS EVALUATION
(Tests for Effective Teaching)

1. Did I reach my goals? Did the members of the group participate in conversational prayer and enjoy it? Was Jesus' presence real to them? How many prayed aloud for the first time?

2. Were sentence prayers unstructured and simple? Were they brief . . . to the point? Were people free to pray more than once?

3. Did I listen to remarks group members made after the meeting . . . to each other . . . to me?

4. Did I commit this session to God and leave the immediate results with him, refusing to suffer inadequacy and inferiority?

5. I will remember that I am planting seeds—introducing new ideas. All will bear fruit in God's time, so I will rejoice and give thanks.

✤   ✤   ✤

From the above questions you should find much about which to pray, both for the members of your group and for yourself. You may find weak spots which need to be retaught or reemphasized.

You will also find much for which to give thanks. When the atmosphere has been right and people have understood what to do, the thank-you prayers have come thick and fast, often with more deep feeling and tears than the situation has seemed to demand. A great deal more has taken place within hearts than anyone can ever know, because we have been in the presence of the Lord our God.

GROUP EVALUATION*

Use the questions that follow as part of your own evaluation of your teaching and the group session. After several sessions, when members are getting the feel of Steps III and IV and finding freedom to reveal their needs and to pray for each other, share the questions with the group.

1. Did you claim the promise of Matthew 18:19, 20? Did you agree together? Did you give thanks together?

2. Were the prayers simple and brief?

*This evaluation should also be used with Chapter 7, Step IV. See "Instructions" in Chapter 7.

3. Did you give the group the reason for not going around the circle to pray? (It places pressure on people, and we want everyone to feel relaxed and quiet and to speak only when the heart prompts them.)

4. Was your group new to each other? Did you use name tags so they felt more at ease and could pray for each other by name?

5. Did you pray briefly for the silent ones by name? (This makes them feel included.)

6. Were requests personal? Were they specific? Did people ask for what they believed God could do for them *now*?** Did they affirm one another?

7. Were faith and love projected by those who gave prayer-response?

PERSONAL NEEDS REVEALED
in a single workshop

The following lists are made up of prayer requests given in a single workshop session. Conversational prayer opened the way for these people to reveal their real needs to others.

From one group:
  patience with children
  love for a neighbor
  strength to face things in life
  not to be so disorganized
  to learn to love my in-laws better
  to be more childlike
  to know God's love personally

From another group:
  for physical healing

**For further teaching on this point see "The Prayer of Asking" in Chapter 7.

    for patience
    for several broken relationships
    for right decisions for her children
    for a daughter in college
    for God's goals in all of us
    for a stronger faith
    for the healing of another

From a third group:
    mother-in-law needs God's help in loving
    guidance in being a Sunday school teacher
    healing power
    forgiveness
    to understand people I work with
    to understand my family
    to be able to pray audibly
    need to accept people as they are
    need to accept my mother-in-law
    need to be less critical
    need to share with others

From these requests we can see the great contrast between traditional and conversational prayer. In traditional prayer there are two main groups of characters: the masked players who are not known and not loved; the judges who are not lovers.

In conversational prayer there is no separation between pray-er and listener. Nor are there any masks to hide us from the judges—there are no judges. We are able to take off the masks, to pray personally, to reveal our needs. We are able to pray for one another by name because we are learning to know each other. We may touch one another. We learn to love one another.

CHAPTER REVIEW
(for the leader first—for the group, later)

1. *How do the following
   subjects*   *affect us?*

   prayer-response
   agreeing
   affirmation
   absolution
   confession
   admission of need
   childlikeness
   expectation
   honesty
   forgiveness
   touch
   addressing one another (#10)

2. What else did you learn?

3. Have the group write out their answers to these and share
   them aloud in groups of four.

SUPPLEMENTARY READING
for Chapter 6

Two or Three Together by Harold W. Freer and Frances B. Hall (New York: Harper & Row, Inc., 1954) is a very helpful book. See especially pp. 62-63 on sharing problems and sins.

Another excellent book is *The Miracle of Dialogue** by Reuel L. Howe (New York: Seabury Press, 1963). The following quotations from this book express the value of dialogue and the importance of being personal in conversational-prayer.

"Only as we know another and are known by him, can we know ourselves. This is the source of the child's knowledge of himself when at last he is able to say 'I,' with consciousness of himself as a distinct, autonomous but related person of worth. Likewise, the mature person is enabled to say 'I' out of his knowing and responding to others." (p. 39)

Question: "We might wonder why it is important for a person to be able to say 'I.' Does it not have a self-centered, if not selfish sound?"

Answer: "Our answer is that if we are concerned about self apart from our responsible relation to others, our concern can be selfish; but when selfhood and the saying of 'I' is prized for the sake of the possibility of dialogue with others, then his affirming the personal pronoun becomes the act of a man's spirit. . . . The principle of dialogue . . . [is] openness to the other side, with a willingness not only to speak but to respond to what we hear." (pp. 39-40)

"Monologue . . . is not only unable to breach the barriers to a meeting of meaning but even creates them because it does not take the other person seriously. In monologue, communication becomes only a juggling of opinions." (p. 44)

Chapter 7

✜ ✜ ✜

STEP IV—HELP MY BROTHER
THE POWER OF INTERCESSION

Jesus answered them, Have faith in God! For I assure you, whoever says to this mountain, "Be taken up and thrown into the sea!" and entertains no inner doubt, but believes that what he says will happen, it shall be so for him.

I tell you, therefore: Whatever you ask in prayer, believe that you received it and it shall be yours. And whenever you rise to pray and you have grievance against anyone, forgive, so that your Father in heaven may forgive you your trespasses.

—*Mark 11:22-25* (Berkeley)

✜ ✜ ✜

"And I tell you once more that if two of you on earth agree in asking for anything it will be granted to you by my Heavenly Father."

—*Matthew 18:19* (Phillips)

WHAT IS INTERCESSION?

To intercede is to act between parties with a view to reconciling their differences. In the Biblical sense, intercession is prayer made on behalf of someone else for the other person's best good. It is an act of love in which the intercessor names the person before God—sometimes with a specific request for God to do a specific thing for that person, at other times just asking for God's love.

Jesus himself is the great intercessor for all of us. The book of Hebrews teaches us about this aspect of his work—his love, concern, sympathy, and help for us (see especially Heb. 7:25). John 17 records the prayer of intercession Jesus prayed for his disciples and for all of us just before his death.

The Holy Spirit, who is one with the resurrected Jesus (II Cor. 3:17), comes to help us in our weakness of not knowing how to pray. Read Romans 8:26, 27 in *Good News for Modern Man* (Today's English Version, published by The Macmillan Company).

Elsewhere in the New Testament we are specifically commanded to pray for others (I Tim. 2:1, Eph. 6:18, 19).

WHAT ABOUT ANSWERS?

Although Jesus taught us that if we asked, we should receive (Matt. 7:7-11), most of us have found that we don't always get what we have asked for—even when we ask on behalf of another. Part of the problem is that we are uncertain as to whether we have asked only according to our own desires, or whether our request is according to the will of God.

I would like to make two suggestions to help you in this area of doubt.

When you pray for yourself: Pour out all your heart's desires. Our Father is love and he is interested in all the details
of your life. As you tell God your desires, you will discover
that things have a way of sifting themselves out, permitting
you to receive God's answer through circumstances. Then be
quiet and wait, confident that God is at work.

When you pray for others: "The Prayer of Love" and "The
Prayer of Blessing" taught in this chapter will help you become
quiet and open to find the "mind of God" for another. But
always remember that you are not the judge, nor the accuser,
nor the arbiter of another's fate. Never confess another's sins
before the Lord God—only your own.

There are other areas of doubt in this matter of prayer.
Some of us wonder: Will God actually grant our request? But
as we look back at requests we have made of God, aren't we
glad that he didn't give us everything we asked for? He has
laws and principles to uphold; he has other lives to consider
besides ours. At the same time, he gives us more of his love,
his care, his concern, than we deserve—of this I am abso-
lutely confident.

Jesus promised us that God will give good things to those
who ask him (Matt. 7:11). But often the things we ask for
are really not in our best interests or for our ultimate good.
So there is always the definite "no" answer. Paul experienced
this kind of answer (II Cor. 12:7-9). I read recently that
God sometimes says *No,* and other times he says, *Well, OK,
have it your way then!* When we receive that answer, we may
discover that we really didn't want what we were asking for.

An even more basic doubt is expressed by many people
who doubt God's love for and interest in us. Is God even
listening to us—do our prayers touch him at all? Does he
care, and if he does, why doesn't he do something?

C. S. Lewis suggests in *Letters to Malcolm* (chapter 11),
that the answers to all these doubts is one of faith. Different
people possess different levels of faith. We are told by Jesus

Christ that God does hear us, that he is listening to us pray. In fact the whole Bible assumes this to be true (see Heb. 11:6). But for some of us it is a great struggle to believe this basic fact. Other people do believe that God is listening, that he hears their prayers, but they have no assurance that he will in fact grant their requests. There are others, however, who pray as God's fellow workers, "demanding what is needed for the joint work"; they find their "confidence justified by the event."

"The difference, we are told, between a servant and a friend is that a servant is not in his master's secrets. For him, 'orders are orders.' He has only his own surmises as to the plans he helps to execute. But the fellow-worker, the companion or (dare we say?) the colleague of God is so united with Him at certain moments that something of the divine foreknowledge enters his mind. Hence his faith is the 'evidence'—that is, the evidentness, the obviousness—of things not seen."*

There is one more thing to be said about answers to prayer. There is the answer God in his love has planned which at the moment seems to be denial of the request, but when quietly accepted—knowing we have the Giver, if not the gift—turns out to be like a million-dollar gift, so far does it exceed any of our asking or thinking.

WHAT IS FAITH

If the answer to our doubts about prayer is faith, how does one increase his faith? Actually, the answer to our doubts is *not* faith. It is love. Yet faith and love are found together.

How to increase love . . .? How to increase faith . . .? Learn of Jesus.

---

*C. S. Lewis, *Letters to Malcolm* (New York: Harcourt, Brace & World, Inc., 1964), p. 61.

For a more complete discussion of this question, read chapters 8 through 10 in my first book, *Prayer, Conversing with God*. Here, just let me say that faith is not hooked up to degrees of desire or of desperation. Faith is that degree of belief we possess in the person of Jesus Christ himself.

In the healing recorded in Mark 5, Jesus says, "Daughter, your faith [that is, your trust and confidence in Me, springing from faith in God] has restored you to health" (Mark 5:34, Amplified). Wherever Jesus uses this phrase, "Your faith . . . has made you whole," you are correct if you insert these two words—*in Me*. Learn more about Jesus Christ, increase and grow in the knowledge of him, and your faith will grow like a mustard seed.

Thy gifts, alone, cannot suffice
Unless Thyself be given;
Thy presence makes my paradise,
And where Thou art is heaven.
—CHARLES WESLEY

INSTRUCTIONS

STEP **IV**
HELP MY BROTHER

Goals: To be channels of God's love and blessing.
 To ask in agreement, one petition at a time.
 To ask in faith and with thanksgiving.

✤ ✤ ✤

1. Acquaint yourself with the four kinds of intercessory prayer described in this chapter.

2. Select the kind of prayer you wish to introduce immediately following Procedure #16 (from Step III).

3. My suggestion would be to teach the prayer of love. Leave the other three for later sessions. Even a brief time spent on the prayer of love will make a lasting impression on members of the group and encourage them to make it a part of their own prayer life.

4. What about *evaluation?* Be sure to include this at the end of each session. Repetition is both necessary and helpful as we learn by repetition and by feedback. Turn to the suggestions at the end of Chapter 5 (group evaluation for Steps I and II) and use them again. With the new and added experience of Steps III and IV, the group should have more to share.

5. Add this evaluation question: What do you like about this kind of prayer as compared to the old way?

6. The evaluation questions in Chapter 6 should first be used by the leader after the session. In later sessions they should be shared with the group when they are ready or need further teaching.

✤ ✤ ✤

This is the last teaching lesson, both in the book and for

the group. In future sessions, go through all four steps without a break, except when it may be necessary to give very short instructions to establish new habits or to discourage continuation of old ones. And you need only a sentence or two to give instructions.

How long should one use the dry-run outlines for the four steps? Until they are so familiar that every person in the group can use them. The order of the four steps will often shift around. (See the section on creative worship in Chapter 9 for variations on Step I, *Jesus is here,* which are suitable for advanced groups.

FOUR KINDS OF INTERCESSORY PRAYER

There are many kinds of intercessory prayer and many ways of praying. There are four, however, which particularly lend themselves to group prayer, and these are the four we will learn in this chapter.

The Prayer of Love. This is a one-word prayer—only the first name of my brother. I give him God's love and mine without asking for anything.

The Prayer of Blessing. This is a one-sentence prayer: Lord, bless my brother—but the content of the blessing is freshly defined.

The Prayer of Asking. Here two or more persons agree on a specific request for a specific situation. It also involves distinguishing between the ultimate goal of the request and the very next step of its fulfilment.

The Prayer of Receiving. This is a prayer of thanksgiving in anticipation of God's answer and involves holding a mental picture of what God is going to do.

The Prayer of Love

Jesus himself is our example for this kind of prayer. In Mark 10:21 we read of the rich young ruler that "Jesus beholding him, loved him." When this young man could not follow the directions that Jesus gave him, Jesus did not condemn, nor scold, nor reproach—He loved him.

DESCRIPTION

For us, the prayer of love is a means of intercession by speaking only the name of my brother, without any request. I bring my brother to Jesus to be loved.

OUTLINE

Love is the first requisite—giving God's love and mine.

The prayer of love is an attitude not an asking.

In Jesus' presence, remembering the four ways he loves me, the overflow of his love for me is for my brother.

I must hold a mental picture of my brother.

I must learn the discipline of love's concentration.

PROCEDURE

1. Have the group members stand in a circle of love, touching hands or shoulders, symbolizing the love and unity of believers. The following directions are for you to give the group as they pray.

2. Open your mind to God's love for you. Remember the four ways God loves you (see Meditation, ch. 4). Let your heart silently expand in gratitude and overflow with the abundance of God's love. Jesus is here!

3. Open your mind to God's love for your brother.

   a. Mentally see this person surrounded by the love of God, His light, warmth, caring, acceptance. Jesus is there, with your brother, too.

   b. Say your brother's name aloud. Concentrate on him

and hold the concept of God's love all around him. Others will be saying the names of their friends.

c. Another person's name will then come to you. Repeat it aloud and mentally affirm God's love around the person, within him, before him, reaching him everywhere. Do this both before and after you say his name aloud.

d. Let God's love flow into you and out to that person, no matter how many miles or how many concrete walls seem to separate you.

e. You are not asking for anything—you are only a channel for God's love. Learn the discipline of concentration.

TIME

Five minutes in a group is enough to spend on the prayer of love. The concentration is short but powerful.

OCCASION

Use the prayer of love any time you are alone, as well as in a conversational prayer group. Use it also to prepare your mind for the prayer of asking (to be discussed later in the chapter).

The Prayer of Blessing

The precedent for this prayer is again from the life of our Lord. "And they brought young children to him that he should touch them. . . . And he took them up in his arms, put his hands upon them, and blessed them" (Mark 10:13, 16).

DESCRIPTION

For us to pray the prayer of blessing means that we call on God's love and wisdom to give our brother what he needs, not what we think he needs (see Rom. 8:27, 28).

OUTLINE

Actively project God's will.

Take hands off—no telling God what to do.
Trust God's love and wisdom.
Employ mental concentration.

PROCEDURE

The directions for praying the prayer of blessing are from Reginald Goff's book *Prayer—an Exciting Adventure.**

1. *Lord, bless my brother*—this is the prayer to be prayed either silently or audibly. The word *bless* here means, "Lord, give to my brother the things that you in your wisdom and love see that he needs." Be specific and name your brother— "Lord, bless our pastor"—"Lord, bless Bob and Grace"— "Bless Stafford."

2. Take hands off and stop telling God what, when, or how.

3. Further state (to yourself) that you recognize your inability to know all about that person or his situation.

4. At the same time, hold a mental picture of the person (the teachable part—the little child within) in the arms of Jesus receiving his blessing. Concentrate on this picture.

5. Clearly affirm in your mind (not audibly) your belief in God's wisdom and love for that person, and in his ability to give to that person what he is planning for him.

TIME

In a group, take from 5 to 10 minutes for using the prayer of blessing.

OCCASION

Use the prayer of blessing in both private and group prayer. Use it also, along with the prayer of love, to prepare in you the quietness necessary to receive the mind of God through the Spirit for the prayer of asking and agreeing. Not until we have given love freely in prayer, and acknowledged our ina-

*(1621 Andros Pl.) Tucson, Arizona: Prayer Unlimited, 1968, pp. 25, 26.

bility to know what to ask, are we ready to begin audible asking for ourselves or for others.

The Prayer of Asking

We are encouraged to pray this prayer by Jesus. "Ask and it shall be given you. . . . For everyone that asketh receiveth" (Matt. 7:7, 8). "If two of you shall agree on earth as touching any thing that they shall ask, it shall be done for them of my Father" (Matt. 18:19).

DESCRIPTION

In the prayer of asking we are led by God's Spirit to ask specifically, not generally, for that which we believe God can do now.

OUTLINE

Face the problem (Mark 11:23).*
Ask in the Spirit (Rom. 8:26, 27).
Make faith-sized requests (Mark 9:24).
Distinguish between the goal and the next step.
Agree and affirm each request made in dialogue prayer.

PROCEDURE

1. Honestly face your problem(s) calling it by its true name to yourself. Admit it to be the mountain it really is blocking your road (Mark 11:23).

2. Pray the request, don't tell it to the group first. The Spirit gave you faith to make the request—He spoke to you as you faced the problem. If you merely tell it rather than praying it, you risk dissipating faith.

3. Leave all negatives—the sins and faults of others, the details of situations—out of the prayer. Be positive. State

---

*See the last section of this chapter for a discussion of the importance of mental pictures as an aid to intercession.

what you believe God can and will do in this situation. Ask boldly.

4. Distinguish between the final goal of your request—that is the ultimate result of what you are asking God to do—and the very next step. Ask for that next step; it will be given to you. It could take place now, today, tomorrow. Believe it. See it mentally.*

5. Immediate prayer-response in dialogue prayer is important. Agree or add to the request just made. Do it without preaching or giving testimony or advice. Do it with faith by giving thanks with love and blessing. Each single petition is important. Not one should go without prayer-response.

6. Remember: Faith is your active mental attitude in God's power and presence.

Faith is your belief in Jesus Christ's power to answer.

Faith is touching Jesus yourself.

Faith is letting love flow like a river.

TIME

As long as you need.

OCCASION

1. Use the prayer of asking when the group is small enough so that people are not embarrassed to pray about their real needs. If you need to, break the group into fours to pray for personal requests (Steps III and IV). Come together again for community requests and more thanksgiving.

2. Use it when the group is without strangers, so that all may freely and confidently participate without fear.

The Prayer of Receiving

The prayer of receiving is based on Jesus' promise to us,

---

*Here you might want to give some direction on the importance of mental pictures from the last section of this chapter.

his disciples: "For every one that asketh receiveth; and he that seeketh findeth; and to him that knocketh it shall be opened" (Matt. 7:8). Jesus also said that "if two of you shall agree on earth as touching any thing that they shall ask, it shall be done for them of my Father which is in heaven" (Matt. 18:19).

DESCRIPTION

The prayer of receiving is essentially a prayer of thanks—prayed in advance of receiving the answer to one's request in actuality. The giving of thanks is the courtesy extended when a gift has been or is about to be received. You will find that when a group agrees in prayer according to the will and purpose of God, the spirit of spontaneous thanksgiving will come upon them. For the use of hands in this kind of prayer, see "The Importance of Touch" in Chapter 9.

OUTLINE

Claim the promise.
Picture the answer.
Give thanks.

PROCEDURE (directions to be shared with the group)

1. Let us claim the promise that if we ask we shall receive (Matt. 7:7, 8). We do this by giving thanks for the answer God is going to give us.*

2. Do not wait for a "feeling" to offer thanks. We are to actively practice what Paul taught in Philippians 4:4-7. As soon as we have stated our request we (with others agreeing) begin at once to give thanks . . .

3. . . . unless others in the group continue in the dialogue of intercession, asking and making requests on the same subject before the thanks is given.

4. We need to be sensitive to the Spirit in our praying, not

_____

*The importance of giving thanks is taught in Chapter 5. Giving thanks as part of the asking is taught in Chapter 6, dry-run #'s 4, 10, 11.

run ahead. Generally the order will be asking, then agreeing, then affirming, then thanking.

5. The picture in your mind as you pray the prayer of asking is that of the mountain falling into the sea with a great splash, leaving cleared ground. As you give thanks, picture your situation changed, the person healed, the answer given. Give thanks each time memory flashes the request. You do not need to ask again. Trust the love and wisdom of God who is already at work in your behalf.**

TIME
As long as you need.

OCCASION
Use the prayer of receiving always when the group has prayed the prayer of asking. Use it in your private prayer also.

MENTAL PICTURES AND INTERCESSION

When a woman cleans house or rearranges furniture, she usually has an idea—a picture in her mind—of how the result of her work ought to look. A business man can see potential in a wavering firm, so he buys it. An architect has a mental picture of the finished building he is designing, and draws up his blueprints accordingly.

These are illustrations of something all of us do every day at home or in the office. We all have pictures in our mind's eye of how things ought to be or could be, and we usually act accordingly.

This faculty of visualizing mentally can be employed in prayer, as an aid to intercession. It enables us to be led by

---

**Reread the section on mental pictures that follows. You will find helpful ideas to share with your group and to use in your prayer times.

the Spirit in our asking and those who use it will be richly
rewarded.

But isn't this rather mystical or psychic? asks someone. Is
it Biblical to pray on the basis of your imagination?

Yes, it is Biblical. Jesus taught us to make mental pictures.
Read Mark 11:22-24. There Jesus told his disciples to picture
the moving of a mountain into the sea—to picture it without
doubt and it would happen. Each person who came to Jesus
to be touched and healed saw himself whole again even before the miracle took place—read Mark 5:28; 10:46-52.

The mountains that confront you and me are not made of
earth and stones. They are all the impossible situations we
are in—that we cannot change or move—that no one can do
anything about. They are made of doubt or unbelief, of lack
of security, of rejection, of loneliness, of financial loss, of
strained or broken relationships, of haunting failure, of painful memories, of physical or mental suffering, of hopeless
living. Today's popular song, "Living is what we do while we
wait to die," characterizes many people. But not the Christian.

And yet, supposing that is our attitude. How can we change
it? How can we get rid of our mountains? For one thing, we
must keep the mountain in view. "There is always hope,"
wrote C. S. Lewis, "if we keep an unsolved problem fairly
in view; there's none if we pretend it's not there."* It isn't
enough to put things "into God's hands." I struggled hard in
my early Christian life to learn to do that—but then it became
a blind refuge for me, a subterfuge of not facing up to the
problem. I've had to learn the balance between facing my
responsibility and trusting God to work it out in his way.

What is your mountain? Don't pretend it isn't there. Don't
rationalize and call it by another name. Face it openly. And

*C. S. Lewis, *Letters to Malcolm* (New York: Harcourt, Brace
& World, 1964), p. 59. Lewis actually had in mind the problem of
fitting unwieldy facts into a consistent philosophical theory—but the
statement holds equally well for any problem that faces us in life.

then speak to it. Speak in authority. Jesus encourages us to call it by name and tell it to disappear into the sea. Picture it moving, falling into the sea, leaving behind the large open space for God to fill. Or, to change the metaphor, tell the problem to *drop dead*. In Christ's presence no power can harm us (Rom. 8:31-39).

LEADER'S PRE-CLASS AFFIRMATIONS

These prayer-thoughts will strengthen your faith, quiet your nervous apprehension, and reassure you of God's love.

1. Recall and pray for each person in your group by name.
2. Let God's love be given to them through you.
3. Visualize their participation. Who will be most apt to co-operate? Who will resist? Why?
4. Draw the resister in with love. See him with the light of Christ surrounding him, penetrating him, filling him.

Repeat these affirmations out loud:
• I will be open to the Holy Spirit to give me sensitivity to each person in the group.
• I will be open to new ideas as I go along, whether they come from the Spirit within, or from the least likely member of my group.
• I will trust God, who is present, who loves each one as He loves me, to give me words.
• I will move in quietness and assurance that this lesson will be presented in love.

SUPPLEMENTARY READING
for Chapter 7

Book and Page	Subject
II pp. 111-118 (ch. 14)	"The Responsibility of Love"
II pp. 66-71 (ch. 8)	"Even If We Doubt, We Can Pray"
II pp. 72-77 (ch. 9)	"We Can Pray, Despite Intellectual Doubts"
I p. 26	Pray by subjects
I pp. 68-73 (ch. 10)	"What Are Faith-sized Requests?"
II pp. 119-125 (ch. 15)	"Praying for Others"
III pp. 55-60 (ch. 6)	Receiving answers

Two other books I highly recommend as valuable tools in the hands of group leaders. Both provide aids for the group as well as meditations for worship and heart-searching growth. They are:

Growing in the Life of Prayer by Harold Wiley Freer (New York: Abingdon Press, 1962).

Two or Three Together by Harold Wiley Freer and Frances B. Hall (New York: Harper & Row, Inc., 1954). This is a manual for prayer groups.

PART III

❖ ❖ ❖

Guidelines

for Growing Groups

Chapter 8

✤ ✤ ✤

HOW TO START A GROUP

"Go home and start a prayer group for young mothers."

This message came insistently to Mary Woodall, a Methodist minister's wife. She had just come from an Ashram* experience where God's healing power had renewed her spiritually and physically.

"I had felt the need for such a group before my healing," wrote Mary, "but now it became urgent. The question a young woman in my Sunday school class had asked me several months previous still haunted me. *Is there a prayer group with a nursery for young women with children?* she had asked. The answer had been negative. At that time I was not interested in prayer groups and did not want to get involved.

"Now, returning from the Ashram, the first news I heard

Ashram is a word borrowed from India. It means a retreat led by a spiritual leader who, with his followers, withdraws from the activities of life for a period of time. Dr. E. Stanley Jones introduced Christian Ashrams to the United States; they are held in almost every state of the union.

was that this young woman was divorcing her husband. Would she have been able to find God's answer to her marital problems in a prayer group? Yes, I'm sure the story could have been different."

In answer to prayer, Mary soon found one interested person to help her. Together they agreed upon a few necessary details. They selected a time and a place, and found a babysitter. Who should be invited? They decided that each was to ask one other person whose name would "come to them" during a time of meditation.

MARY TELLS THE STORY

"There were five of us when we first met. We shared our limited spiritual experiences and prayed. The day soon came when there were 12 of us. That day we knelt in the sanctuary together with a distinct sense of awe and wonder. It was a high and holy experience. Each one of us committed ourselves and our group to Jesus Christ anew.

"For almost a year nothing spectacular happened. We did find new strength and faith for ourselves, but our prayers didn't seem to be making much difference in the lives of those for whom we were praying. We seemed to be saying prayers rather than praying.

We Learned to Pray Conversationally

"One day, two of us brought the same book to the meeting on the same day! It was Ros Rinker's book, *Prayer—Conversing with God*. We read it through chapter by chapter and claimed the promise of Matthew 18: 19, 20, as she taught us to do.

"We also followed these suggestions:

1. Speak directly to the Lord Jesus.

2. Pray by subjects, one at a time.

3. Pray conversationally . . . back and forth on a single subject until thanks comes spontaneously.

"A great simplification came. We were honestly talking with the Lord. We were so conscious of his presence, it was as though actually he were right there with us.

"Then another book came to us—Dr. Leslie D. Weatherhead's *Private House of Prayer.** From him we received a framework** for our conversational prayers. This outline is taken from the list of titles used for devotional readings in Part III of Dr. Weatherhead's book.

1. Affirm the presence of God.
2. Look at God: praise, thank, adore.
3. Confess and unload.
4. Receive forgiveness.
5. Petition for self.
6. Intercession for others.
7. Meditation and dedication.

"When we first started our prayer group, we would talk 45 minutes and pray for 15 minutes. Conversational praying and the above framework made a great difference. We reversed our procedure! Instead of wasting our energy and time, we dispensed with the spiritual gossip, and did our talking directly to the Lord instead of to each other.

"We found ourselves praying from an hour and a half to almost two hours—without stopping. Even then no one wanted to go home, so close was the bond of love and unity between us.

Miracles Happened in Our Lives

"We began to operate in full power, however, only after

---

*New York: Abingdon Press, 1958.

**Since then the framework for conversational prayer used in this book has been worked out: four Basic Steps with only three words in each step, but including the seven parts of Dr. Weatherhead's framework. (See Chapter 2.)

we discovered the power of regular daily devotions in our own lives.

"A whole new dimension in living began to operate within us which we recognized as the power of the Holy Spirit.

"We grew in understanding God's will for ourselves, our church, and our world. A sense of mission was given to us. Love and faith put us to work: a kind deed here, a word of love there, a telephone call, obeying a hunch, a visit to a friend or neighbor at just the right time, temper controlled, love for a former enemy, new concern for world needs, an awareness of spiritual poverty in our church, the necessary will-power to stop smoking or to go on a diet. These and many more blessings flooded in upon us.

"We began to see almost immediate answers to our prayers. Physical healings, spiritual commitments, and even mental healings took place. We saw fresh results in our church, in our minister. The dissension in our board was cleared up. A men's prayer group was started. Prayer meeting in the church on Wednesday evenings are now broken up into seven groups: four adult groups, a Senior High group, a Junior High group, and a children's group."

SEVEN STORIES FROM THE GROUP

"One day in church, our minister's wife invited me to join a prayer group which was to meet on Thursday. I thanked her and wondered what a prayer group was. I had no intention of going, but thank God, I did!

"I'd been to a few church prayer meetings, but only out of a sense of obligation. I didn't even know how to pray aloud. Me? Pray those beautiful, long, dignified prayers? I didn't do much praying anyhow. Little did I know that all I had to do was just talk to God. I found out that's what prayer really is—talking to God."

—J

✤ ✤ ✤

"Five years ago, my only son—handsome, wonderful, fine —took his own life. The shock sent me to a mental institution for seven months, but Mary's group began to pray for me and to send me notes of love and encouragement. Soon my memory was restored, and I was released. About two months after my return home, one day on my knees I experienced complete spiritual and physical healing. Great peace and freedom has come to me—freedom from anxiety, fear, selfishness, resentment and self-pity. More than this, God has given me a new mission in life. Now, every teenage boy or girl I see, is mine and God's. My heart goes out to them in love and prayer, and He helps me find ways to become a friend to them."

—F.

✤ ✤ ✤

"I worshiped my beautiful new home until I joined the prayer group. I am no longer a slave to that house, but glad and ready for any orders the Lord gives me each day. My migraine headaches have ceased. The story of how my husband accepted Christ and joined the church is a real answer to prayer."

—M.

✤ ✤ ✤

"Within a period of 18 months I experienced the agony of going from sublime happiness to the depths of despair. I became pregnant with our second son. My husband started drinking excessively, his income disappeared, he joined the army, deserted, and has never been located. Then my mother suffered a cerebral hemorrhage and in ten days was gone.

"I developed a diabetic condition with complete physical and mental exhaustion. Due to a malignant gum condition, all my teeth were extracted. I almost lost my sanity, but God stepped into the picture. Just as I turned on the gas to commit suicide, the thought came, *Ask God to forgive you and to take care of the children.* I dropped to my knees in prayer— I have no idea how long. I seemed to see Jesus with his arms outstretched, saying, *Come to me with your weakness, and I will give you rest.* He took me in his arms, reassured me, and then said, *Return to your children, and remember, I am with you always.*

"Today, I still have problems, but the difference is that now I know God is with me, and if he can be for me, who can be against me?"

—V.

A minister's wife shared her deep concern with the group. Due to financial pressures and a son in college, her husband felt forced to give up his church and take a job. They had learned not to tell God what to do, but simply give themselves to him, that "his will be done" in their lives. Two months later he was called to pastor a brand-new church. The light has returned to his eyes, and his wife is radiant again.

"Our home life was a nightmare. My desperation made me humble and willing to join Mary's group. As a result, both my husband and myself have found God's love and our own love renewed. Life is worth living again."

—M. B.

"My mind was so full of myself that a nervous condition affected my throat. One day as I was hanging up clothes, and giving thanks, God spoke, 'Margaret, you are not ready to be completely healed yet—you have many things to learn.' I started to cry at the overpowering realization that God had spoken to me. I also had an inferiority complex because I am so small of stature. As I stood there, I became aware of a tiny tree near me, filled with fresh growth. Suddenly I realized that I, too, could grow in God's love, that he loves me just as I am. My mind is at rest, and I can now pray for others in faith."

—M. H.

GUIDELINES FOR A PRAYER MEETING

As the group continued to meet they developed a number of guidelines, both on how to conduct the meeting and on how to pray. Mary shares them here with us. As you read them, remember that although the group was composed mainly of housewives, the principles God taught them are valid for everyone.

Mechanics of the Group

1. Give this meeting priority. Attend every week unless a sick child with fever prevents.
2. Begin and end at the exact time agreed upon.
3. Eliminate all "small" conversation preceding the meeting.
4. The program must contain prayer, Bible study, and sharing (or witnessing) in order to be a dynamic channel for the work of the Holy Spirit.
5. The nursery: Each girl will contribute 25¢ per child for one and a half hours. The place of the group meeting must be "way-far-away" from the nursery.

Praying for Ourselves

1. The Lord Jesus is a member of our prayer group. We talk to him, share with him and with each other.

2. Sharing in the group must be honest. Release comes more quickly when we confess our sins "one to another" (James 5:16). All confession does not have to be aloud, for in silence our Lord hears and answers.

3. We never share with others outside the group what is said in the group—not even with our husbands!

4. We pray for one another and love one another. Our love grew until complete harmony prevailed almost every time we met.

5. Should harmony be lacking:

At least two of us would always sense it at once if any one member was in mental turmoil. If more than one member was in distress and unable to share, it seemed as though it was like riding wild horses to keep the group centered around our Lord Jesus. Those who felt the tension learned to deal with it silently in prayer.

Silently, we directed God's love and peace toward that person. Then we concentrated on her for a period of time—until we felt the tension relaxing. It was amazing how harmony was restored to the entire group. That person might never know what went on, but those of us who prayed knew, and God knew.

Praying for Those Not Present

1. We pray daily for each other, our church, our ministers, and persons on our prayer list.

2. We give that one to God, by directing God's love to him. We put him into God's hands. Then we visualize the need actually being met. From that moment, we never ask again. Whenever we are reminded of this person, *we give thanks*, even when we see no evidence of visible results.

3. Praying for one very ill or beyond our reach: We direct our prayers to the subconscious mind of that person. This really works. It works with sleeping children, too.

4. We do not tell people we are praying for them, unless they have specifically asked for our prayers.

SUPPLEMENTARY READING
for Chapter 8

Book and page   *Subject*

HOW TO BEGIN

I   p. 78 (#6)   Five steps for beginning to pray
I   pp. 21-23 (ch. 3)   Simple prayer language
I   p. 29   Fresh beginnings
I   pp. 40-43   Reasons for praying aloud together
II   pp. 106-110   Breaking the sound barrier
I   pp. 48-53 (ch. 7)   Suggestions for daily devotions
I   pp. 76-83   13 suggestions for praying together
III pp. 51-52   Reevaluation of church prayer life
III pp. 40-41   Love begins with one person
III p. 111   How "The Followers" began
III pp. 113-114   An offshoot of "The Followers"
III pp. 124-127   More pointers on how to begin
III pp. 16-17, 122-123   Changing from a traditional prayer
                              meeting

HOW NOT TO BEGIN

I   pp. 25-26   Avoid round-the-circle prayers
I   pp. 44-45   Barriers (a summary)
III pp. 15-21 (ch. 1)   "Why I Don't Attend Prayer Meet-
                              ing"
III pp. 41-42   When love is missing
III pp. 71-76 (ch. 8)   Excuses (and how to overcome
                              them)

AFTER YOU'VE BEGUN

III pp. 108-113   "The Followers" and their program
III pp. 114-118   Interview with the organizer
III pp. 99-102   "Re-search Groups" and their out-
                              reach
I   p. 77   Balanced use of group time
HB   Check the index under Evaluation

Chapter 9

✤ ✤ ✤

LEARNING WHY
WE DO CERTAIN THINGS

UNDERSTANDING PEOPLE'S REACTIONS

We must always be aware that there are people who will not accept change readily, especially a change involving prayer. They will oppose any new method of praying because they do not understand it. And it is true that change is not really necessary for them; they may continue "their kind of prayers" in private and with their friends.

What such people should realize, however, is that with new tools comes a greater flexibility, allowing us to reach people. This is particularly true in relation to those who cannot pray audibly but who are open to the simplicity of conversational prayer. Not only in prayer but in every area of Christianity we need to be aware of new approaches and not permit familiar traditions to become stumbling blocks.

In Salem, New Jersey, one strong-minded woman left the group called "The Followers"* for three years. She didn't un-

---

*Described in Book III, chapter 12.

derstand the third step of conversational prayer, *Help me, Lord*. She thought it meant public confession of all one's sins. What it really means is that we are to be open-hearted so others will know how to pray for us. Eventually this woman returned to be part of the group. Now she thanks God for conversational prayer.

Then there is the friend in Arizona who rejected my presentation of conversational prayer the first year I was there. She felt near to God when she prayed long prayers, and she thought I was against long prayers. I'm not—I pray them myself when I'm alone or with one or two. There is a time and place for everything.

The following year, she attended a briefing session in leadership training with 50 other people, and suddenly the light dawned. Short prayers help new believers! Short prayers open up seeking hearts! Now she understands why people stopped coming to a prayer group she had started.

In a Christian Ashram held in Florida, two Cuban teenagers who were in my classes picked up this teaching on conversational prayer. Rebeca and Lupe went back to Miami Beach and began teaching it in Spanish to women in cottage-meetings. They had many invitations to teach people to pray and were enthusiastic about results.

They wrote: "Conversational prayer in groups works miracles! We know because we have experienced them. When people pray for someone else's need, they forget their own problems, and then their own needs are met! At the same time it gives a sense of security to the person who is being prayed for—the security of knowing she is not alone, that another person cares, and even greater than that—that Jesus loves her too."

"Change the way I pray?"
Listen to the dismay and the underlying pain in that ques-

tion. It is hard to change a pattern we have been using for so long. Yet if we would stop and think, we would discover that we do not always pray in formal language. As I said in Chapter 2, when we are alone or working or traveling or driving, our private prayers *are* conversation with God. It is when we pray for the ears of others, in the presence of others, that we become very righteously religious—our prayers full of well-known and accepted phrases, yet so impersonal and often so cold and rigid.

Why do we resist change? In change there is new vitality, new life, freshness, power. New life, however brings growth and growth can mean pain. All of us resist pain. Yet while it is painful to change, it is even more painful to resist change. If we could only see that when we do open our hearts to change, courage will be given to us—courage to face ourselves and share ourselves, even to love ourselves.

The sin of religious people today is that of being unresponsive to the fresh evidences of the Spirit who is sweeping out the old and bringing in the new.

HOW TO HAVE A SPIRIT-LED GROUP

QUESTION:
We want a group which is Spirit-led and Spirit-filled. Can you give us some guidelines or tests?

ANSWER:
I believe in the filling of the Spirit. I have observed, however, that experiencing his filling in some special way does not make us perfect so that we are unable to sin. Nor do such experiences automatically make us able to love one another. We need more than one dramatic experience—rather we need the Holy Spirit's continuing presence, his indwelling.

The Holy Spirit indwells people who have opened their

whole being to Jesus Christ, who willingly give up their personal rights—to be obedient and to operate their lives by faith and love.

That is to say, God's Holy Spirit fills every container (the Bible uses the phrase *earthen vessel*) available to him. Not that we can contain him in any great measure. We receive as much of the Spirit as we are able to contain. The more of ourselves we give to him as growth and experience continue, the more of himself we are able to receive.

Group Leadership

The way to have a Spirit-led and Spirit-filled group is not to depend on some special experience, or on some enthusiastic leader. The responsibility for group leadership is located in the member-leaders who are committed to Jesus and have received the new life of the Spirit. When each member of the group has such goals, any person attending who has not committed his life to Christ will, in all probability, experience this commitment *within himself* during his first visit. Be sensitive to this possibility and even expect it.

Marks of the Spirit's Guidance

It is not possible for me to mention all the situations in which you may find the Holy Spirit prompting you inwardly on how to lead a group. But I guarantee that as you are open to his guidance, you will be doing things you never heard of before—things you have not read in this book or any other book—things that will work toward edification, enlightenment, clarification, spiritual and physical healings, the lifting of burdens, and above all the glorifying of Jesus Christ our Lord.

In a Spirit-led group, there will be:
- joy and laughter as well as tears
- asking and agreeing by name and by project

LEARNING WHY WE DO CERTAIN THINGS

- laying on of hands for special prayer
- joining of hands for faith and unity
- breaking off prayer in order to share
- singing of a hymn or chorus
- asking for things thought impossible
- praying by name for those present
- praying by name for those absent
- receiving guidance to sit, kneel, or stand; to break into groups of twos, threes, or fours; to make a telephone call; to visit a friend or neighbor; to obey a hunch; to control one's temper at home; to love a former enemy; to end an argument; to give up one's rights; to stop trying to change someone; to go on a diet; to get the proper amount of rest; to read the Bible; to give a word of love; to entertain a stranger.

You will be amazed at the guidance of the Spirit into some procedure which soon becomes a part of your group activity. This can be exciting, especially when later you find others who are being led in the same direction (John 15:13-15).

The Gift of Wisdom and of Teaching

We cannot structure or harness the Holy Spirit. That is to say no amount of study can determine what he will do in a meeting; no amount of practice of conversational prayer will guarantee his presence.

I am not saying that I do not believe in adequate study and preparation. I certainly do. But study in itself is not enough. After all the planning there is the need to be flexible and sensitive to the Spirit. Only he knows the needs of the persons in the group. Only he can give us the wisdom to meet those needs and the ability to teach people the things they need and want to know.

The needs of persons present are more important than any plans we might have made. People are more important than programs. So let us ask for the Holy Spirit's gift of wisdom and teaching.

CREATIVE WORSHIP FOR ADVANCED GROUPS

Variations for Step 1 (Chapter 4)

After you have the devotional ideas from the dry-run outline of Step I *(Jesus is here)* well in hand, heart, and participation, you will probably find new ideas for your meetings springing up from varying sources. To start you thinking about possible additions or changes in your praying I am suggesting some variations for your consideration.

You will need to turn to the dry-run outline for Step I as you study this section, but the time consumed will be well worthwhile. Look especially at #'s 7-13.

#7 Jesus in our midst.

#8 Visualizing him—a painting, his hands.

#9 Being a little child—near him.

#10 Recognizing his presence.

#s 11, 12 Words he wants us to hear.

#13 Words we want him to hear.

Study these for a moment and you will see that most of them are word-pictures. Lesson I has used them all at one session. It might, however, be wiser and simpler to select two which go well together and use only those at the first meeting and for several weeks until they are very familiar. Then for subsequent sessions select alternates and so redirect the group's thinking and meditation and enlarge their creativity in prayer. You might use one old one and add a new one. Or use only new ones. Whatever you do, pray over your selections. Then trust the Holy Spirit to guide you. Often I don't know which one I'm going to use until I'm right there with the group and sense what is needed. That is the Holy Spirit's task—to meet our needs, to mold us into one circle, one body, one family, one kingdom.

For possible variations, try these.

1. Revelation 3:20. The open door, the open heart, a meal with Jesus.

2. Mark 10:13-16. Being little children, blessed by Jesus.

3. Mark 1:30-31. Put yourself in the place of Peter's mother-in-law.

4. Make your own selections from the Bible. Use a story from the life of Jesus, a parable, or a few verses of his teaching which create a mental picture. (John 8:12 or 15:3-4 are possibilities.)

When you present any of these alternates, remember that only a few well-directed words are necessary to paint a mental picture when your hearers are listening with their eyes closed.

We must learn to use the faculty of imagination, which is God-given, to help bring the unseen God into the personal world of reality. The more we exercise our imaginations in this capacity, the more real Jesus becomes and the more we love him. Thus our prayer life becomes more rewarding and more practical.

Meditation Dramatization

The dry-run outline for Step I used four phrases about the way God loves us taken from a meditation which appeared in Book II and which is also available in card form.* An effective dramatization of this meditation was worked out at Hickam Air Force Base in Honolulu in 1967, using as well the dialogue that precedes the meditation.**

❖ ❖ ❖

SCENE: *stage decorated with a few pots of green plants and some artificial flowers, and a garden bench. Dim*

---

*See pp. 49, 52, Chapter 4.
**Book III, pp. 103-104.

audience lights, have a spotlight for the stage (if possible).

1. *(Empty stage)* Music: "In the Garden."

2. Girl comes on stage, quietly sings first verse and chorus of "In the Garden" from memory, then walks off.

3. Second girl comes on stage, picks a flower, sits down on the bench, puts face in hands, looks up and begins the dialogue.

4. Male voice off-stage, using a mike, takes the words of Jesus in the dialogue. Voice should be very quiet and assuring, speaking the words clearly. Voice closes with the complete meditation.

✧   ✧   ✧

Using the dialogue and meditation in conversational prayer, having two or more people reading the parts, is also effective. It helps give a sense of the presence of our Lord, making him real to us.

TO LISTEN UNDERSTANDINGLY

(as people pray)

The suggestions which follow are by Bobby Jones from Wainwright House. You will find that they will make you a sympathetic listener, if you will put them into practice, and will enable you to pray with understanding and love for group members.

Give these suggestions to your group at some meeting after they have been using Steps III and IV a few times.

✧   ✧   ✧

Listening involves three distinct, active steps, says Bobby Jones.

1. *Keep out of it.*

That is, keep yourself removed as you listen to people pray for themselves. Keep objective. Don't intrude physically, verbally, or mentally by thinking about yourself.

Shut up and listen.

To do this is hard. It is not a passive, but a positive attitude.

2. *Listen. Don't plan what you are going to say.*

Don't think you can interrupt. Don't think how to solve the problem you are listening to, how to admonish, how to advise, how to solace. Don't think . . . listen.

3. *Understand what is being felt as well as what is being said.*

Hear every nuance of tone and meaning. Listen to intent as well as content. *Listen.* Put yourself in his shoes, at his point of reference, at his state of understanding.

THE IMPORTANCE OF TOUCH

The importance of touch is a subject of growing significance these days. It is a subject people are either for or against. There is a wrong way to use one's hands, but is that any excuse for failing to use them in a right way?

"Jesus made use of the power of touch simply because it was right," states Ralph Osborne.* "His hands, reaching out to a person in need were sacramental. He was incarnating what He felt and what He said *by what He did.* Compassion was what He felt. God loves you, is what He said. And the touch of His hand confirmed both as true."

People sought to touch Jesus, and he touched them. As a result, they were healed and helped (Mark 1:31; 5:23, 41; 6:2; 8:23, 25).

In how many life situations does touch convey the meaning more clearly than words! It is hard to think of any in which

*"The Amazing Power of Touch," *Open Circle,* November, 1968 (Faith at Work, New York).

this is not true. Today many of us are watching and evaluating the activities sponsored by Sensitivity Groups which seek to promote the healing of inter-personal relationships.

What do you do with your hands? How can hands be used to make prayer more effective? Long before I ever heard of sensitivity groups, I began to teach the use of hands and was amazed at the results.

"Feeling follows action rather than precedes it," wrote William James. Act, and the feeling will come. The dry-run outlines in this book are based on this premise. Try it yourself, in any kind of a life-situation, as well as in prayer.

Use your hands to pray in the following ways:

1. *For recognition* of an individual as a person. As you join hands for a circle-of-love (Step I), the meditation *God loves you* very soon becomes a double-header: God loves you and so do I. "This is the first time anyone ever touched me in any way except to shake my hand after a meeting," said a brother in Honolulu, as he gratefully expressed what that circle had meant to him.

2. *For a sense of quietness.* Hands folded together in prayer, or held with palms together, give one a bodily sense of quietness and expectation—a readiness to ask (Ex. 17:11, 12).

3. *For preparation.* Half of Christendom uses the right hand to make the sign of the cross at the beginning or end of a time of prayer. Are you aware of the significance of this action?

4. *For offering praise.* Hands uplifted from the shoulder express praise and worship. The American Indians used this gesture as they prayed with eyes wide open.

5. *For personal need.* Hands extended together at waist level, palms turned up express both offering and petition. Try doing this for Step III or Step IV when some depth-request is presented, or when special caring is called for. The gesture coincides with our words and gives our faith a boost: "Lord,

here is Paul . . . we lift him to you on hands of faith . . . for *your love and your blessing* (and any added petitions)." Standing in a circle this is very effective, and thanksgiving quickly follows.

6. *For person-to-person agreeing.* When prayer is accompanied by deep concern (with tears) ask the person to hold his open hands out (as in #5). Let three or four others place both hands under his, thus giving the visible illustration of the undergirding of agreeing-prayer. This expression gives comfort and brings thanksgiving (which is the first receiving of the answer).

7. *For showing concern and belonging.* When a group member "chokes up" and cannot continue, let those nearest him quietly place a hand on his shoulder—and let the gesture be continued all around the group, making an unbroken circle of contact. The action expresses our attitude: that our faith and our caring are joined in agreement for God's *love and blessing* in his situation. This agreement can be given both silently and audibly.

8. *For healing* of the spirit, mind and body. The early church practiced laying-on of hands and anointing with oil (James 5:13-16; Acts 6:6, 9:12, 17; 19:6). It is gratifying to see that most churches have laid aside prejudices regarding this practice. A special gift is given by the Holy Spirt to some people for this ministry. However, a group may practice the laying-on of hands for any member requesting spiritual or physical healing. The faith of the person calling for the laying-on of hands seems to be part of the point of contact which brings the answer. Prayer-by-proxy is possible, as the one requesting prayer for a loved one sits in his (vacant) place, while others lay their hands on his head and pray for him.

In conclusion, there are many motions the hands can make—to express praise, petition, concern, or to portray mental concepts. May we be open and teachable to that free-

dom of expression in mind and in word which the hands portray, thus making it possible to give our highest service to
God and to each other.

PRAYERS: WRITTEN OR SPOKEN?

In this book on teaching others the simplicity of conversational prayer, I knowingly ran the risk of offending people
who object to written prayers. Their objection is that written
prayers foster formalism and hinder the Spirit from giving
free expression as we pray.

After years of free expression in prayer, I have finally discovered the *Book of Common Prayer*. A fine balance of mental concentration and satisfactory worship has become my re-
ward as I follow the prayers for Morning or Evening Worship
and for Holy Communion. Even the free forms of prayer have
taken on more depth of meaning, not less, because I use these
written prayers.

C. S. Lewis (long one of my favorite authors) in *Letters
to Malcolm* has made thought-provoking remarks about the
need for written words.* Mr. Lewis aptly calls words *anchors,*
however they are used. "The choice between ready-made
prayers and one's own words [is] rather less important for me
than it apparently is for you. For me, words are in any case
secondary. They are only an anchor. Or, shall I say, they are
the movements of a conductor's baton: not the music. They
serve to canalize (i.e. to channel) the worship or penitence
or petition which might without them—such are our minds—
spread into wide and shallow puddles. It does not matter very
much who first put them together. If they are our own words,
they will soon, by unavoidable repetition, harden into a for-

---

*C. S. Lewis, *Letters to Malcolm* (New York: Harcourt, Brace &
World, 1964), p. 11.

mula. If they are someone else's, we shall continually pour into them our own meaning."

The written prayers in this book are for instruction as well as for usage, mainly to show the utter simplicity which the heart requires for reality. You do not need to quote nor follow verbatim those prayer-words; you may freely reword them, or change them. I only ask that you retain the childlike simplicity which characterizes their present form.

Whoever you are
God can use you if you will let him
to be a teacher of prayer.

BIBLIOGRAPHY

✣ ✣ ✣

INDEX

SELECTED BIBLIOGRAPHY

❖ ❖ ❖

I. FOR GROUP STUDY

A. Bible Study Material

Howard, Walden. 52 *Weeks With the Bible*. New York: Faith at work, 1965 (25¢ each, 10 for $2.00. Order from Faith at Work, P.O. Box 1970, Waco, Texas 76703.) Studies from the Old and New Testaments that will encourage depth encounter. Ask for their magazine.

————. *Group Encounters With the Bible*. New York: Faith at Work, 1967. (25¢ each, 10 for $2.00. Order from Faith at Work, P.O. Box 1970, Waco, Texas 76703). Studies primarily from the New Testament on the meaning of the Christian life.

Peace, Richard. *Learning to Love*. Vol. I: *Learning to Love God*. Vol. II: *Learning to Love Ourselves*. Vol. III: *Learning to Love People*. Grand Rapids: Zondervan Publishing House, 1968. ($1.00 per volume, or $2.75 for 3-volume set.) Fresh workshop material. Highly recommended.

Rinker, Rosalind. *Who Is This Man?* Grand Rapids: Zondervan Publishing House, 1960. (Paper $1.50.) 15 studies in the Gospel of Mark using the inductive method and detailed teaching help. Purpose: to know (the deity of) Christ and to believe on him.

Schell, Catherine and Marilyn Kunz. *Neighborhood Bible Studies.* (Write for sample study and manual at $1.25 to Box 222, Dobbs Ferry, New York 10522.) These studies from both the Old and New Testaments are widely used on the East Coast. They are effective and personal, designed for home and group study combined, using the inductive method.

B. Books on Prayer

Freer, Harold W. *Growing in the Life of Prayer.* New York: Abingdon Press, 1964. Contents closely parallel the four basic steps of prayer taught in this handbook. A bibliography includes books up to 1961.

Freer, Harold W. and Frances B. Hall. *Two or Three Together.* New York: Harper & Row, Inc., 1954. One of the best manuals for prayer groups in print. It includes a complete bibliography, in outline form, of both classic and modern books on prayer up to and including 1952.

Hamilton, H. A. *Conversation With God.* Nashville: Abingdon Press, 1961. ($1.75.) I carried this book with me on lecture tours for a whole year. Short, vital, Christ-centered instructions and meditations.

HIS Magazine *Conversational Prayer.* (25 pamphlets for $4.00. Order—prepaid only—from His Reprints, 4605 Sherwood, Downers Grove, Illinois 60515). Reprint of magazine articles introducing and teaching conversational prayer.

Radcliffe, Lynn J. *Making Prayer Real.* Nashville: Abingdon Press, 1952. (Paper $1.25.) A group in Toledo, Ohio, highly recommends this book.

C. Rosalind Rinker's Books on Prayer

Book I. *Prayer—Conversing With God.* Grand Rapids: Zondervan Publishing House, 1959. (Cloth $1.95. Paper 60¢.) The story of conversational prayer. Suitable for readers of all ages and stages.

Book II. *Communicating Love Through Prayer*. Grand Rapids: Zondervan Publishing House, 1965. (Cloth $2.50. Paper 75¢.) Assists in locating barriers to love. Gives brief instructions on group prayer.

Book III. *Praying Together*. Grand Rapids: Zondervan Publishing House, 1968. (Cloth $2.95. Paper 95¢.) An analysis of the lacking elements in most prayer meetings. Suitable for those who desire change.

D. On Life and Relationships

Day, Albert. *Discipline and Discovery*. Nashville; Parthenon Press. (Paper 65¢.) A small but powerful book.

Larson, Bruce. *Living on the Growing Edge*. Grand Rapids: Zondervan Publishing House, 1968. ($2.95.) A resource book for restless individuals and groups, with depth questions.

_____. *Setting Men Free*. Grand Rapids: Zondervan Publishing House, 1967. ($2.95.) Ten chapters on the arts and gifts needed by those who reach to others in an outgoing witness.

Mow, Anna B. *Your Teen-Ager and You*. Grand Rapids: Zondervan Publishing House, 1967. (Cloth $2.95. Paper 95¢.) For young parents—a powerful book on how to love.

_____. *Your Child*. Grand Rapids: Zondervan Publishing House, 1964. (Cloth $2.95. Paper 95¢.) How to raise your children and teach them to love God. Mrs. Mow speaks from experience as the mother of four, now grown.

Radcliffe, Lynn J. *Making Prayer Real*. See under Prayer, I, B.

II.   DYNAMICS OF GROUPS

Brayton, Anthony and Marjorie. *Prayer Group Guide*. (Booklet, 10¢. Order from Camps Farthest Out, 1569 Grand Ave., St. Paul, Minn. 55105.) A reference guide of suggestions from prayer groups of Camps Farthest Out.

Deshler, Byron. *The Power of the Personal Group*. (Paper 35¢. Order from Tidings, 1908 Grand Ave., Nashville, Tenn. 37203.) Twelve studies for small groups.

Emerick, Samuel. *A Manual for Prayer Groups.* (Order from The Upper Room, 1908 Grand Ave., Nashville, Tenn. 37203.)

Goff, Reginald. *Prayer: An Exciting Adventure.* Tucson, Arizona: Prayer Unlimited, 1968. (Order from 1621 Andros Pl., Tucson, Ariona 85705.) Chapter 2 discussses dynamics and depth with helpful suggestions.

Howard, Walden, editor. *Groups that Work.* Grand Rapids: Zondervan Publishing House, 1964. (Paper 95¢.) A handbook for laymen and churches compiled from articles in *Faith at Work* magazine.

Howe, Reuel L. *The Miracle of Dialogue.* New York: Seabury Press, 1963. (Cloth $3.50. Paper $1.95.) Examines principles rather than method. Contrasts dialogue with monologue—helping in practicing conversational prayer and in teaching communication, as well as in personal encounter through groups.

Johnson, Ben C. *Learning to Pray.* Atlanta: Lay Renewal Publications, 1966. ($1.00.) Personal experiences, exercises, helps for starting a group.

Morris, Danny E. *Wanted: Ten Brave Christians.* Atlanta: Spiritual Life Publishers, 1965. 27-page pamphlet.

————. *A Life That Really Matters.* Atlanta: Spiritual Life Publishers, 1965. 110-page book. Both of Mr. Morris's works tell what happened to the first 38 people who followed the Five Disciplines in Tallahassee, Florida.

Pert, George and Florence. *The Small Group.* Carmel, New York 10512: Guideposts. (25¢ each; 6 for $1.20.) This 18-page pamphlet contains fresh practical material.

Rogers, Harold. *The Twelve.* (Order from Tidings, 1908 Grand Ave., Nashville, Tenn. 37203.) This 15-page pamphlet describes a group-centered program which changes lives. An adventure in discipleship.

Taylor, Alice J. *Starting the Prayer Group.* Cincinnati: Forward Movement Publications, 1959. (Order from Forward Movement, 412 Sycamore St., Cincinnati, Ohio 45202.) The author is the wife of an Episcopal clergyman.

Yokefellows staff. *New Dimensions in Spiritual Growth.* (Paper 50¢. Order from Yokefellows Inc., 209 Park Rd., Burlingame,

Calif. 94010.) Directions on how to start and lead a Yoke-fellow group for the first eight sessions.

III. PRAYER

Allen, Charles L. *Prayer Changes Things.* Old Tappan, N. J.: Fleming H. Revell, 1964.

Boyd, Malcolm. *Are You Running With Me, Jesus?* New York: Avon Books, 1967.

Bloom, Anthony. *Living Prayer.* Springfield, Ill.: Templegate Publishers, 1966.

Carruth, Thomas A. *Total Prayer for Total Living.* Grand Rapids: Zondervan Publishing House, 1962. Discusses the group in the church and in the family.

Day, Albert E. *An Autobiography of Prayer.* New York: Harper & Row, Inc. 1952.

Johnson, Ben C. *Learning to Pray.* See under II.

Laubach, Frank C. *Prayer, the Mightiest Force in the World.* Old Tappan, N. J.: Fleming H. Revell, 1946.

————. *Letters by a Modern Mystic.* Old Tappan, N. J.: Fleming H. Revell, 1956.

Lewis, C. S. *Letters to Malcolm: Chiefly on Prayer.* New York: Harcourt, Brace & World, 1964.

Lockyer, Herbert. *How I Can Make Prayer More Effective.* Grand Rapids: Zondervan Publishing House, 1953.

Prayer: Its Deeper Dimensions. A Symposium. Grand Rapids: Zondervan Publishing House, 1963.

Quoist, Michel. *Prayers.* New York: Sheed and Ward, 1963. Depth prayers to promote inner healing—poignant, personal, revealing.

Shoemaker, Helen. *The Secret of Effective Prayer.* Waco, Texas: Word Books, 1968.

Thielicke, Helmut. *Our Heavenly Father.* New York: Harper & Row, Inc., 1960. Studies in the Lord's Prayer.

Weatherhead, Leslie D. *A Private House of Prayer.* New York: Abingdon Press, 1958.

Whiston, Charles. *Instructions in the Life of Prayer*. Cincinnati: Forward Movement Publications. (412 Sycamore St.) Depth studies from the Book of Common Prayer.

IV. RELATED SUBJECTS

A. The Deity of Jesus Christ

Bickersteth, Edward H. *The Trinity*. Grand Rapids: Kregel Publications, 1957. A detailed Scriptural and theological presentation.

Carnegie-Simpson, P. *The Fact of Christ*. London: James Clark & Co., 1952. (Paper.) A contemporary book for students, setting forth the claims of Christ.

Price, Eugenia. *What is God Like?* Grand Rapids: Zondervan Publishing House, 1960. Easy reading, a case well presented.

Rinker, Rosalind. *You Can Witness With Confidence*. Grand Rapids: Zondervan Publishing House, 1962. Chapter 11 gives verbal and non-verbal claims to Christ's identity.

_____. *The Years That Count*. Grand Rapids: Zondervan Publishing House, 1958. Chapter 3: What do I believe about God? Chapter 4: What do I believe about Jesus Christ?

Rinker, Rosalind. *Who Is This Man?* See I, A.

B. God's Love and Presence

Day, Albert E. *An Autobiography of Prayer*. New York: Harper & Row, Inc., 1952. Chapter 6: What a vivid consciousness of God does. Chapter 7: How one becomes God-Conscious.

Elliott, Norman K. *God Really Loves You*. St. Paul, Minn.: Macalester Park Publishing Co., 1954. (3 for $1.00) Everyone should read this.

Larson, Bruce. *Setting Men Free*. Grand Rapids: Zondervan Publishing House, 1967. Chapter 9: The Gift of Love.

_____. *Dare to Live Now*. Grand Rapids: Zondervan Publishing House, 1965. Chapter 4: Learn to Love.

Lawrence, Brother. *The Practice of the Presence of God*. Cincinnati: Forward Movement Publications. A classic. This is available in several other editions from other publishers.

Peace, Richard. *Learning To Love God*. See I, A.

Raines, Robert. *The Choice of Love*. New York: Harper & Row, Inc., 1959. You may have to go to a library for this, but it's worth the trip.

Rinker, Rosalind. *God Loves You/God Is Always Near You*. Recording by Word Records, Waco, Texas. 1968. (W-6152-LP) For acceptance and love.

C. Confession

Bonhoeffer, Dietrich. *Life Together*. New York: Harper & Row, Inc., 1954. Chapter 5: Confession and Communion, is excellent.

Dixon-Smith, H. *Discipline for Life-Changing Service*. India: U.S.C.L., 1939, out of print. Chapter III. The Discipline of Confession.

Drakeford, John. *The Awesome Power of the Listening Ear*. Waco, Texas: Word Books, 1967. Chapter 16 on confession discusses integrity, theology, and Dr. Hobart Mowrer.

Freer, Harold Wiley. *Growing in the Life of Prayer*. See I, B. Chapters 8-12 discuss confession.

Goff, Reginald. *Prayer—an Exciting Adventure*. See II. Pages 32-35 discuss receiving forgiveness and forgiving yourself.

Johnson, Ben C. *Christian Involvement*. Atlanta: Lay Renewal Publications. (Paper $1.25.) Page 29: Effective Communication.

Larson, Bruce. *Dare to Live Now*. See IV, B. Read Chapter 11 if you are asking: "Why be honest?"

Lewis, C. S. *Letters to Malcolm*. See III. Chapter 8 discusses prayers of anguish. Chapter 4 discusses confession and being a person.

Miller, Keith. *The Taste of New Wine*. Waco, Texas: Word Books, 1967.

———. *A Second Touch*. Waco, Texas: Word Books, 1967. Both of Mr. Miller's books discuss the need for honesty about ourselves and in personal relationships.

Peale, Norman Vincent. *Sin, Sex and Self-Control.* Carmel, N. Y.: Guideposts, 1965. Chapter 11: The Twilight of Honesty. Chapter 12: Blow the Dust off Your Standards.

Quoist, Michel. *Prayers.* See III. Pages 109-145: Stages of the Road.

Whitlow, Brian. *Hurdles to Heaven.* New York: Harper & Row, Inc., 1963. Plain talk on seven root sins. The last chapter, The Way Back, is a fitting climax to the book.

D. Intercession

Augsburger, Myron S. *Invitation to Discipleship.* Scottsdale, Pa.: Herald Press, 1964. Chapter 9: The Victory of Depth Prayer.

Day, Albert E. *An Autobiography of Prayer.* See III. Chapter 19: Observations on Intercession.

Lewis, C. S. *Letters to Malcolm.* See III. Chapter 11 discusses why petitions are refused, and degrees of faith.

E. Meditation and Worship

Dunlop, M. V. *Stillness and Strength.* Guilford, England: Fellowship of Meditation, 1963-64. Studies in contemplative meditation.

Goldsmith, Joel S. *The Art of Meditation.* New York: Harper & Row, Inc., 1956.

Teilhard, de Chardin, Pierre. *Hymn of the Universe.* New York: Harper & Row, Inc., 1961.

Underhill, Evelyn. *Worship.* New York: Harper & Row, Inc., 1936.

V. CHURCH RENEWAL

Bonhoeffer, Dietrich. *Life Together.* See IV, C. A classic on community encounter.

Carruth, Thomas A. *Total Prayer for Total Living.* See III.

Casteel, John L. *Spiritual Renewal Through Personal Groups.* New York: Association Press, 1957. The story of eight church fellowship groups.

Gilmore, Don G. *In the Midst.* Grand Rapids: Wm. B. Eerdmans, 1962. A Methodist church.

Monro, Claxton and William S. Taegel. *Witnessing Laymen Make Living Churches.* Waco, Texas: Word Books, 1968. Stories from an Episcopal and a Presbyterian church in Houston, Texas.

Morris, Danny E. *A Life That Really Matters.* See II. The story of John Wesley Methodist Church, Tallahassee, Fla.

O'Connor, Elizabeth. *The Company of the Committed.* New York: Harper & Row, Inc., 1963. The story of the Church of the Saviour in Washington, D. C.

Raines, Robert A. *New Life in the Church.* New York: Harper & Row, Inc., 1961.

Index

✛ ✛ ✛

INDEX TO SCRIPTURE REFERENCES